WORLD FAMOUS
TRUE LOVE STORIES

WORLD FAMOUS
TRUE LOVE STORIES

Colin and Sally Wilson

Constable & Robinson Ltd
3 The Lanchesters
162 Fulham Palace Road
London W6 9ER

This edition published by Magpie Books,
an imprint of Constable & Robinson Ltd 2005

A copy of the British Library Cataloguing in Publication Data
is available from the British Library.

ISBN 1 84529 010 0

Printed and bound in the EU

Contents

Chapter One

Paris and Helen of Troy

Until fairly recently, Helen of Troy was regarded as a completely mythical character.

This is hardly surprising, since, according to the Greek legend, Helen was the result of an irregular union between a beautiful princess called Leda and a swan – who was actually the god Zeus in disguise. Far from being indignant at the discovery that she had been impregnated under false pretences, Leda seems to have acquired a taste for this peculiar form of sexual gratification, and went on to bear Zeus the twins Castor and Pollux.

The legend says that Helen was the most beautiful woman in the world. In fact, her attractions were apparently irresistible when she was merely ten years old. The hero Theseus – who was also the King of Athens – saw her when he was on a visit to Sparta (Leda was the wife of the King of Sparta) and tossed a coin with his friend Pirithous to decide which of them should have her. They carried her off when she was dancing in the Temple of Artemis.

What happened next depends on which poet or historian you prefer to believe. Plutarch says that Theseus did not marry Helen because she was too young, but left her at a small town called Aphidna in the care of his mother Aethra. But an earlier version, which accords better with Theseus's well-known taste for deflowering virgins, declares that she became pregnant by him and had a daughter.

The legends seem to agree that her brothers Castor and Pollux set out to rescue her, and probably sailed with an army, since they are said to have conquered the city of

Athens. The Athenians claimed that they knew nothing about Helen, or where Theseus had taken her. Then a man called Academus – probably anxious to get rid of the brothers – told them that she was in Aphidna. This was also attacked and captured. Helen was taken back to her home in Sparta, and Theseus's mother Aethra was taken along as a prisoner.

This adventure made Helen so famous that dozens of suitors flocked to Sparta to ask for her hand. Her father Tyndareus apparently decided that she was too young to choose for herself, and examined the suitors one by one. Before he would even accept them as possible candidates, he made each of them swear that, whoever became Helen's husband, the others would all go to his aid if he was ever attacked by enemies. Finally, Tyndareus chose Menelaus, the younger brother of Agamemnon, King of Mycenae, and not only gave him his daughter, but also yielded up his throne to him.

For two or three years, Menelaus and Helen seem to have lived together happily, and Helen gave birth to a daughter called Hermione. Then a visitor named Paris arrived from Troy – on the coast of what is now Turkey – laden with rich presents. Menelaus entertained him hospitably, failing to realize that Paris had come there with the specific intention of stealing his wife.

At this point, we have to digress to explain why Paris was willing to take this considerable risk. The legends about him are just as absurd as those about Helen. He was the son of King Priam of Troy, but a few days before his birth, his mother Hecuba had a horrifying dream in which she gave birth to a blazing torch, which burned down the whole city. She was so shaken that she decided to kill the baby by exposing him on Mount Ida. The child was found by a shepherd, who called him Paris, and brought him up as his son. Paris also became a shepherd, but his natural dominance made him a leader among the shepherds of Mount Ida.

Apparently he was also placed in charge of cattle, for when King Priam needed a bull to be given away as a prize in some funerary games, it was Paris who brought the finest bull in all the herds on Mount Ida to Troy. Here he took part in the games, and carried off all the prizes, defeating his brothers, including Hector. The brothers were so jealous they decided to kill him. But at this point, he was recognized by his sister Cassandra – she was also a prophetess – and finally took his rightful place as the Prince of Troy.

Paris was as famed for his good looks as Helen was for her beauty. This was to contribute to his downfall for as the most handsome shepherd on Mount Ida, he had once been asked to judge a beauty contest between three goddesses – Hera (wife of Zeus, also known as Juno), Aphrodite (also known as Venus) and Athene (also known as Minerva.) The prize was a golden apple, which had been thrown down by the goddess of discord, Eris, who was angry at not having been invited. All three goddesses tried to bribe Paris – Hera by promising him power and riches, Athene with glory in war, and Aphrodite by offering him the most beautiful woman in the world. Paris decided to accept Aphrodite's offer, and judged her the most beautiful of the three – making the other two goddesses life-long enemies.

The woman, of course, was Helen.

She was happily married, but with the goddess of love on his side, Paris could hardly fail. And when Menelaus made the mistake of going off to Crete, Paris lost no time in persuading Helen to elope with him. He added insult to injury by carrying off most of the gold in Menelaus's treasury.

Menelaus hastened to his brother Agamemnon to complain, and Agamemnon spent the next ten years (another authority says two) assembling more than a

Aphrodite, the goddess of love, persuades Helen to follow Paris

thousand ships and over a hundred thousand men. The force included the suitors who had promised Menelaus help in his time of need.

The story of the Trojan War hardly needs retelling. Troy stood in the middle of a windy plain, and should have been fairly easy to take. But the Trojans had heard about the preparations, and also summoned allies from all over Asia Minor and Thrace. Their attempt to prevent the Greeks from landing was unsuccessful, and the Trojans were driven back into the city. Next, Menelaus tried diplomacy, and offered to withdraw his forces if Paris would return his wife. By this time, Helen seems to have repented of the trouble she had caused, and declared herself ready to return with Menelaus. But Paris refused, and the war went on.

For nine years, the Greeks failed to penetrate the walls of Troy. But in the tenth year, Odysseus (Ulysses) suggested the famous trick of sailing away, and leaving behind a wooden horse, which the inhabitants pulled into the city. The Greeks emerged from it at night, and opened the gates to the rest of their army – which had only sailed over the horizon. And so Troy fell, its men were massacred, its women and children dragged away into slavery, and Helen restored to her husband.

The legend declares that Helen – now homesick – played some part in the downfall of Troy. Odysseus, disguised as a beggar, managed to enter the city – his aim being to steal a statue of Zeus that was believed to make Troy impregnable. Helen recognized him, but helped him to steal the statue – and also agreed to help in causing the city's downfall.

Paris had meanwhile been killed in battle, and Helen had married his younger brother Deiphobus. Helen also betrayed Deiphobus to the Greeks.

Then, according to legend, she returned with her husband to Sparta, and they lived happily ever after. But another tradition declares that, after the death of Menelaus, she was driven out of Sparta by her stepsons, and fled to Rhodes, where she had an old friend called Polyxo. What Helen had failed to reckon on was that Polyxo now hated her, for having caused the death of her husband in the Trojan War. And the most beautiful woman in the world – now an old lady – ended her life swinging on the end of a rope on a tree.

This, then, is the story of Helen of Troy, as told by dozens of poets – the most famous of whom is Homer. But did Troy really exist, or was it a figment of Homer's imagination? For if Troy existed, then in all probability, so did Helen. This seems to be the view taken by the historian Grote, writing in the mid-nineteenth century, who calls his chapter about the war 'The Legend of Troy'. A more recent dictionary of classical mythology agrees that Troy existed, but thinks that 'the so-called siege of Troy really implied the efforts made by Greek traders to break a trade monopoly long enjoyed by the feudal princes of the city'.

It was in the year 1829 that a seven-year-old boy named Heinrich Schliemann received a copy of Jerrer's *Universal History* for Christmas. When he saw the picture of Troy in flames, he was struck by the thought that nothing could possibly destroy such mighty walls. The young Schliemann resolved that he would one day go and investigate the matter for himself. Forced to become a grocer's assistant at the age of fourteen, Schliemann decided to embark for South America as a cabin boy. In 1854, he happened to be in California at the time of the Gold Rush, and it made him rich. (Recent biographical investigation reveals that his methods were thoroughly dishonest.) At the age of forty, he was finally able to realize his ambition to go and search for Troy. Together with his wife – a sixteen-year-old Greek schoolgirl – he sailed for the northern coast of Turkey to begin his search.

At that time, scholars accepted the idea that the remains of Troy would be found on a mountain near Bunarbashi, about three hours from the sea. Schliemann knew his Homer, and disagreed – according to the *Iliad*, the Greek heroes rode between Troy and the coast several times a day. It was true that, in those days, the sea came a great deal further inland, but even so, Schliemann thought Bunarbashi was too far. Instead, he decided to look at a mound called Hissarlik, only about an hour from the sea.

His guess proved to be inspired. When he began digging – in 1871 – he soon uncovered the remains of a town, but it dated from the Roman period, and was only a hundred yards across. Below this was another ruined town. And then another. And then another. Eager to find Homer's Troy, Schliemann ordered his men to slice a great trench through the middle of the mound of Hissarlik, and keep going until they reached bedrock. All told there proved to be the ruins of nine cities, one on top of the other.

Twelve years later, Schliemann announced that he had found the treasures of King Priam – treasures that, for some odd reason, he had always been convinced would still be there. (He never explained why the conquerors had not simply stolen them.) In his autobiography he tells a remarkable story of how he had glimpsed a copper vessel through a hole in the wall, and waited until his workmen had gone to lunch – he was afraid they might be tempted to steal – before he and his wife removed a treasure of drinking vessels and jewellery. These finds were to make him world famous.

In later years, the same biographical research that revealed that Schliemann's fortune was based on lying and cheating the gold miners, also uncovered the fact that the finding of the treasure was also an invention – it had actually been found over a considerable period, and concealed from the eyes of his partners in the enterprise.

7

True Love Stories

The fact remains that his discovery of 'the jewels of Helen' filled the archaeological world with excitement, and inspired generations of archaeologists.

Schliemann moved to Mycenae, and made equally remarkable discoveries there – including a golden mask which he unhesitatingly labelled 'the mask of Agamemnon'. Back on the plains of windy Troy, in 1889, he made a discovery that demonstrated that his archaeological methods were less than perfect. Outside the mound, and well beyond the limits of what he had believed to be Homer's Troy, he found the remains of a large building that in turn contained the remains of pottery that was unmistakably Mycenaean – that is, from the period of the siege of Troy. That meant that he had sliced straight through the Troy he was looking for, and destroyed a great deal of valuable evidence. In the following year, he died of a stroke, collapsing in the street.

Schliemann had been convinced that Priam's Troy was the second from the bottom. He learned too late that this was about a thousand years too old. But which of the other seven was Homer's Troy?

Schliemann's collaborator, Wilhelm Dorpfeld, went on excavating. He came to the conclusion that Homer's Troy was the sixth city from the bottom. This city had immense walls which extended well beyond the mound of Hissarlik, as well as a giant tower which must originally have been sixty feet high.

There was one problem. This Troy had clearly been destroyed by an earthquake. The walls had crumbled, and in one place the foundations had even shifted. But Homer's Troy was supposed to have been burned to the ground.

In the 1920s, an American archaeologist named Carl Blegen concluded that 'Troy six' was not the Troy of the *Iliad*. He thought that it was probably the next one up – which he called Troy 7a. This seemed to be a kind of shantytown, where there had formerly been houses of the nobility, but in which there were now cramped 'bungalows'. Blegen speculated that people who had normally lived outside Troy had crowded into it during the siege. Inside the gate was a building that Blegen called the 'snack bar', a combination of bakery and wine shop where Blegen imagined the Homeric heroes rushing to refresh themselves after battle. Troy 7a *had* been burned – Blegen found smashed skulls, charred skeletons, and an arrowhead. It was this that caused him to announce confidently: 'The sack of Troy is a historical fact.'

His triumph was undoubtedly premature. Archaeology had certainly uncovered a town of roughly the correct date – some time around 1250 BC – and it looked as if this town had been destroyed either by fire or earthquake. But there was still not the slightest fragment of evidence for the real existence of Paris or Helen – still less that they were responsible for the Trojan War.

This evidence was to come from a completely different source.

In 1834, a young Frenchman named Charles Texier was riding through central Turkey when he heard of some ruins near the village of Bogazkoy. They proved to be the gigantic remains of an earlier civilization, with tremendous walls and magnificent ruined buildings ornamented with winged demons and unknown hieroglyphs. It took half a century before it was recognized that these were the remains of a mighty empire that had once extended from Asia Minor down to Syria – the empire of the people known as the Hittites, who had once attacked Babylon. Their empire, like that of the early Greeks, collapsed about 1200 BC; but two centuries earlier it had been one of the greatest nations in the Middle East. The period of the fall of Troy had been the period of the slow disintegration of the Hittite empire. Moreover, most of Asia

Minor had been part of that empire. So Troy was, in a sense, a Hittite town.

The remains discovered by Texier were those of the Hittite capital, Hattusas, and in excavations between 1906 and 1908, the archaeologist Hugo Winkler found a mighty library of clay tablets, some in Hittite and some in Akkadian, the language in which diplomacy was conducted. Deciphered during the First World War, the tablets – from the Hittite equivalent of the Foreign Office – gave a detailed impression of the working of Hittite foreign policy.

In 1924, the Swiss historian Emile Forrer announced that he had found references to a country named *Ahhiyawa*, somewhere to the west, which he identified as meaning 'Achaia-land' – in other words, Greece (Homer always referred to the Greeks as Achaeans, or Achaiwoi).

In 1963, an archaeological dig at Thebes (north-west of Athens) uncovered more Hittite documents dating from the right period. These records revealed that the 'Ahhiyawans' controlled some territory on the coast of Asia Minor, including a city called Millawanda or Milawata. Now on the coast of Asia Minor, some 200 miles south of Troy, there was a Greek-controlled city called Miletus, earlier known as Milatos. Geographical accounts make it clear that Miletus is Milawata. And since the Hittite records refer to the land of the Ahhiyawa as 'overseas' from Miletus, this seems to confirm that Ahhiyawa is mainland Greece. The records revealed that relations between the Miletan Greeks and the Hittites were basically friendly.

They also show that a Greek king was in dispute with the Hittites around 1260 BC – roughly the right date for the siege of Troy. It was about a northern city called Wilusa. We know that the early Greeks called Troy Ilios or Wilios. At about this date, the Hittite king Hattusilis mentions in a letter that he is having trouble with the Greeks.

About ten years later Hattusilis writes to the king of the

Greeks, whom he addresses as 'brother'. It seemed that this king's brother had been causing trouble for the Hittites. What seems to have been happening was this: the brother of the Greek king, a man named Tawagala, had joined with a rebel from Arzawa – a region north-east of Miletus – in harassing the Hittite garrison. The emperor of the Hittites marched with an army to Miletus, found that his enemies had fled, and wrote an angry letter to the Greek 'king' that made it clear that the Greeks were then a major power in the Mediterranean. The king to whom the Hittite emperor was writing could well have been Agamemnon. His rebellious brother Tawagala has been identified as a Greek named Eteocles, and if we knew that Agamemnon had a brother of that name, it would clinch the argument. Unfortunately we only know of his other brother Menelaus.

In the television series *In Search of the Trojan War*, the historian Michael Wood argues strongly that Wilusa *was* Troy, using a great deal of geographical evidence from the Hittite records. Moreover the king of Wilusa is called Alaxandus, and Paris's other name was Alexandros – which means 'protector of men' (which legend claims he received in the days when he was a shepherd). Homer often refers to Paris as Alexandros of Troja. Wood cites other Hittite records that show that the king of the Greeks was in Asia Minor in the reign of Hattusilis III (1265–35 BC – which would include the date of the Trojan War). If that king was Agamemnon – as seems likely from the dates – then we have powerful evidence for Homer's story.

There is another piece of evidence for the existence of the Trojan War, unearthed by Blegen in his excavations at Pylos, the home of Homer's King Nestor. Among the tablets found there were many referring to a large number of 'Asian' women who were apparently slaves, and whose main tasks were grinding corn and preparing flax. Asia, as we already know, was one of the names for Turkey.

Dr Schliemann, the German archaeologist who excavated Troy

Paris and Helen of Troy

References to the places from which these captives were taken make it clear that they came from many places on the north coast of Asia Minor, including Chios and Miletus. The sheer number – 700 women, 400 girls and 300 boys – suggests that they were captives of war. Some of these women are referred to as *toroja* which sounds like 'people from Troy'. Again, the date is right – the period of the Trojan War. No men are mentioned – and Homer tells us that the men of Troy were all killed.

So what the historical record appears to tell us is this. The period of the Trojan War was, in fact, a period of many wars in Asia Minor. The empire of the Hittites was weakening, and the Greeks took advantage of this to raid 'Asian' settlements and to encourage rebellion. Troy (or Wilios) had always been a faithful ally of the Hittites, and records show that the Trojan prince Alaxandus had fought on the side of the Assyrian king Muwatallis. Another independent tradition from south-west Asia Minor declares that the lover of Helen is an ally of Muwatallis. So if this Alaxandus is indeed Prince Alexandros – Homer's Paris – then he was not a young man when he seduced Helen, but a grizzled veteran approaching middle age.

Prince Alexandros – who is probably Paris of Troy – fought on the side of Muwatallis at the battle of Kadesh (in Syria) in 1274 BC. At this time, some great and influential king, who may well have been Agamemnon (or possibly his father Atreus) was on the throne in Mycenae. If these dates are correct, then it must have been about 1264 BC that Alexandros went to call on Menelaus, brother of Agamemnon, in Sparta. We may surmise that Menelaus was not a particularly strong character – legend represents him as unlucky in love and war – and that Helen found the battle-scarred veteran Paris more attractive than her unexciting husband, and eloped with him.

Tristan and Iseult

The romance of Tristan and Iseult and the magic potion that was the cause of their forbidden love and eventual downfall is probably the most famous love story of the western world, which has inspired first troubadours then poets, writers and composers right up to the present.

Seemingly it is just a legend told through the ages, but evidence exists that the adulterous happenings described in this story may have really taken place during the sixth century at a local ruler's court in Cornwall. During the centuries following the tale was passed on by bards and troubadours by word of mouth elaborating the original story but still retaining basic details. When for the first time it was put into writing by the poet Béroul in a poem that has survived to the present day, he included many place names that can still be located in Cornwall today. He named Malpas as the perilous ford, the market at Marazion, the castle of Dinas, and Tintagel as the site of King Mark's summer court. Blancheland, Lantyan, St Sampson's, the forest of Moresk and other more obscure place names that feature in his version of the story can all be found on maps today.

This fact alone would not be enough to prove that the story really did occur in a Cornish setting, but more tangible proof exists in the form of an ancient longstone that still stands beside the road leading to the little port of Fowey. Inscribed in sixth century lettering it states in Latin, 'Here lies

Tristan the son of Cunomorus'. A fragment of the
stone has clearly been broken off and the
inscription recorded in the sixteenth century by the
travelling scholar Leland, who examined the stone
then, includes also the words – 'and the lady
Clusilla'. Now Cunomorus is recorded in other
early documents as being King Mark of Cornwall, a
historical character whose full name was Marcus
Cunomorus and whose territories included a
fortified palace site near Fowey. The name of
Tristan is clear enough on the stone today and if
the name Clusilla is translated into early Cornish it
comes out as very close to Esselt or the French
Iseult.

At the same time recent archaeological
discoveries at Tintagel prove conclusively that in
the sixth century AD it was the site of the summer
palace of an important Cornish ruler. From this
headland he and his followers carried on important
trade by sea with the Mediterranean and Ireland.
Marcus Cunomorus is known to have ruled in mid-
Cornwall during that time and so the poem is
probably correct when it names him as the lord of
Tintagel, and Tristan is named too but for some
reason the poem calls him the king's nephew, not
son.

Why should this be? Well if the real events at
King Mark's summer court included the seduction
of the Irish princess who was his wife by his own
son Tristan, and ended in the death or even
possible execution of these tragic and guilty lovers,
their adulterous liaison and the fascinating story of

intrigue at their own ruler's court might have been retold by the local Cornish people, and passed down through several generations until made into a poem by the travelling bards.

At this point, to make the bardic recitals more seemly, Tristan had to become Mark's nephew instead of his son. The name Tristan becomes Drustan in Cornish and Iseult is really Esselt. Both these personal names are still to be found in Cornwall today, embedded in ancient place names that date from very early times but are not found at all elsewhere.

So perhaps the names carved on the ancient Cornish memorial stone may indicate that the real story of Drustan and Esselt and Mark could have ended in reconciliation after all.

When Menelaus went to his brother to complain, Agamemnon may or may not have been indignant at the abduction of his sister-in-law, but he knew perfectly well that the west coast of Anatolia ('Asia') was highly vulnerable since the Hittites had been forced to go to war with various neighbours, including the Assyrians. And Troy was a wealthy trading centre, famous for its horses. Its position in northern Turkey meant that it was the natural meeting place for the traffic of the Black Sea and the Aegean. Troy, says one classical dictionary, was practically 'a feudal castle to take toll of merchants. From Troy radiated the great trade routes by land; these met the Greek trade route by sea across the Aegean.' So Agamemnon could anticipate rich plunder.

The Greeks attacked Troy, and the Hittites were too weak

to send aid to their allies. But Troy was virtually impregnable, with its massive walls. Besides, the plain was so windy and cold that the Greeks would have found it far too uncomfortable to simply surround Troy and wait until it fell. They beached their ships between two headlands, and protected the landward side with a great wall of earth, timber and stones. It was in this camp that they spent most of the next nine years. So the siege of Troy was less a siege than a series of engagements.

In the tenth year something happened. Wood makes the interesting suggestion that the story of the wooden horse may be a 'folk memory' of the earthquake that destroyed part of the walls, and enabled the Greeks to get in. The sea god Neptune (Poseidon) was often worshipped in the form of a horse, and was supposed to be a master of horses. But he was also the god of earthquakes – perhaps because the trembling of the earth suggests a great stampede of horses.

And so, we may surmise, the siege of Troy ended round about 1254 BC, Helen returned to the arms of her husband, and the Greeks sailed back home. Ulysses spent ten years wandering around the Mediterranean and encountering various adventures before he returned to his wife Penelope, and found her surrounded by eager suitors who assumed he was dead. Agamemnon returned home to be murdered by his wife Clytemnestra (the sister of Helen) and her lover Aegisthus. The contrite Helen returned to Sparta with Menelaus. And Greek bards – who were capable of remembering thousands of lines – commemorated the story in song, and retold it at every feast.

Regrettably, this was the end of the 'age of heroes'. During the next half-century, raiders who were known simply as 'the sea peoples' wreaked havoc throughout the Mediterranean, causing the downfall of Agamemnon's Mycenae, Nestor's Pylos, and the new 'bungalow' Troy that had succeeded the Troy of King Priam. The age of great

True Love Stories

kings and great palaces was over, and Greece and the rest of the Mediterranean plunged into a dark age.

And in due course, scholars came to doubt whether the siege of Troy had ever taken place, and whether Paris and Helen had ever existed . . .

Chapter Two

Alexander the Great

Alexander of Macedon, one of the greatest generals the world has ever known, was worshipped as a god within his own lifetime. He modelled his career on Homer's Achilles, from whom (he was convinced) he was descended on his mother's side. Like Achilles, he was courageous, handsome and almost invincible; also like Achilles he died young (aged thirty-two), a short time after the death of his lifelong friend and lover.

There are several characters in the story of Alexander's life who have become legendary in their own right: the philosopher Aristotle, who was his tutor, his mother Olympias, believed by many to have been a sorceress, who arranged the murder of Alexander's father, King Philip, and Bucephalus his horse, the great black stallion untameable to all but Alexander. Altogether less known is his lover and companion in arms Hephaistion – perhaps because historians have preferred not to emphasize this vaguely scandalous relationship. Yet Hephaistion was the single most important person in Alexander's life: childhood friend, trusted companion, second in command, and the great – perhaps the only – love of his life.

In ancient Greece moderate homosexuality was as openly accepted as sex with wives or mistresses; no one raised his eyebrows if a married man also had the occasional male lover, even a boy. Extreme homosexuality or male prostitution was usually regarded as absurd or abhorrent (Alexander lost his temper with a man who offered to procure him boys), but between two young men, or a young and an older man, affairs were not uncommon. It was thought of as a fashion, not a perversion: part of the learning experience. Most young Greeks would have grown out of their male love affairs fairly early on; in the case of Alexander and Hephaistion, it was strong enough to last for life.

The remote mountainous kingdom of Macedon, in what is now the Balkans, was regarded by the rest of the Greek states as the barbarian fringe. The sophisticated inhabitants of the cities further south laughed at the tough and warlike Macedonians with their thick beards, thick accents and primitive manners. But by 356 BC, when Alexander was born, the city states had been squabbling among themselves for more than a century, and Philip, Alexander's father, saw his chance. What he wanted was to see all Greece united under one power – himself. He saw that then, with the combined Greek armies, he would have a force with which to challenge and conquer the vast rival kingdom of the Persians, who occupied all of known Asia; it was the greatest empire in the world and its wealth was legendary. Philip dreamed of becoming King of Persia.

The dream had started when he was a fifteen-year-old boy, and had been captured by a Greek general and sent to Thebes to guarantee the good conduct of his elder brother King Alexander. It was like going from some small country town to Paris. Philip was dazzled by its sophistication and culture. He was an intelligent youth, and he threw himself into the study of art, literature and philosophy. And when his elder brother was assassinated, Philip returned to Macedon and seized the throne. But after Thebes, he found Macedon a stagnant backwater. He determined to drain off the stagnation and turn it into another Greece. He was a born soldier, and soon converted the Macedonian Army from a disorganized rabble into a magnificent fighting machine. After subduing the hill tribes of his own country, he went on to conquer the lands to the north. Now he was not fighting for power or for territory, but for glory, for the sheer joy of conquest. And, of course, to become worthy of the admiration of the Greeks. Like some medieval knight, he was doing battle for the honour of his lady. And when he had subdued the lands to the north and east, he marched south to conquer the lady herself. Thebes was soon over-run; so was Athens, which prepared itself for brutal punishment for defying Philip. But Philip was not out for revenge; he only wanted to be regarded as a Greek.

And in his moment of greatest triumph, his life was cut short by an assassin within his own court. Philip was in his mid forties and about to celebrate the birth of a child to his new young wife, when he was stabbed to death by a nobleman with a grudge, who was probably put up to it by the estranged Queen Olympias, Alexander's mother.

Suddenly, aged nineteen Alexander found himself faced with the challenge of carrying out his father's ambitious plan. He rose to the occasion with such success that many believed the story told by Olympias, that he was not Philip's son, but the child of Zeus.

From the numerous portraits and from accounts of Alexander's life and deeds it is possible to form a picture of his physical appearance. He was remarkably handsome, with a straight nose, jutting forehead and a full, sensuous mouth. He had blondish-brown hair parted in the middle and swept back, slightly curly, it gathered at the nape of his neck and framed his clean-shaven face. His appearance was in marked contrast to the usual Macedonian fashion for men, of close-cropped hair and large beards. Early on in his career critics commented that he looked effeminate, but within a short time his powerful personality and his achievements had gained such respect that his appearance became the model for all subsequent kings.

Hephaistion was probably about the same age as

True Love Stories

Alexander. He was the son of a Macedonian nobleman and seems to have been brought up and schooled alongside the prince and a group of young noblemen of similar age, who were groomed to become royal Companions – Alexander's bodyguard and trusted advisers. From the only remaining statue, Hephaistion appears to have had short hair and a long straight nose; although not as handsome as Alexander, he had a noble forehead, and was probably taller of the two – he was once mistaken for the king when the two stood side by side.

Even under Philip, the uncultured Macedonian court had become more cosmopolitan. Artists, doctors, philosophers and musicians were drawn there from all over the Aegean world. The teenage Alexander and his companions were taught philosophy, languages, arts, sciences and astronomy under their tutor Aristotle, one of the greatest thinkers of his day. They were also taught horsemanship, battle skills, oratory and strategy: how to fight for and then rule a great empire.

When Alexander set off into Asia to conquer the Persians, he first visited Troy, where he and Hephaistion paid tribute to the Greek heroes of the Trojan War, 800 years earlier. They laid wreaths on the tombs of Achilles and his beloved friend Patroclus – a name by which Hephaistion was sometimes called.

In battle after battle Alexander's troops were vastly outnumbered by the Persians, but the Greek soldiers were so well organized and fought with such determination – inspired by Alexander and his Companions – that they won every battle.

After the battle of Issus in 333 BC, the Persian king Darius fled, abandoning his wife and harem (who accompanied him everywhere) to the enemy. Fortunately, Alexander was always merciful to captives and chivalrous to women (rape was not permitted, even when his soldiers had won a battle). When Alexander entered the Persian queen's tent accompanied by Hephaistion, she threw herself on the ground before Hephaistion, mistaking him for the king. Alexander acted quickly to rescue her from embarrassment, saying, 'No mistake, for he too is Alexander.' After which, he stretched out on a silken couch, and raised his goblet of wine with the comment, 'So this is what it's like to be royalty . . .'

As well as being Alexander's lover and friend, Hephaistion was also a highly successful soldier and leader in his own right; Alexander placed him in positions of power he could entrust to no one else. Before the decisive battle of Gaugamela, Hephaistion went on ahead with half the army, to bridge the Euphrates; when the army faced defeat through the betrayal of one of Alexander's generals, it was Hephaistion who took over command of the all-important Companion cavalry. And after Darius was defeated a second time, when Alexander was setting up a system of government which would incorporate the Persian and Greek systems, Hephaistion became his Grand Vizier and chief minister.

During Alexander's eleven-year campaigns in Asia, the two men were able to spend less and less time together; the endless complications of ruling the vast empire kept them both busy. But finally, after becoming king of Persia, Alexander decided that they should cement their relationship by becoming in-laws. It was typical of the Greek attitude to sex that two male lovers should find nothing contradictory in taking wives – in fact, Alexander had already married a beautiful captive named Roxane. He planned a huge festival at Susa, north of what is now the Persian Gulf, in which ninety or so of his officers would marry Persian brides. He himself would marry two more wives – the youngest daughter of King Artaxerxes, and the eldest daughter of Darius, while Hephaistion would wed her younger sister. In this way he would be uncle to Hephaistion's children.

When he learned that approximately 10,000 of his men had Asian mistresses, he made up his mind to celebrate the biggest wedding ceremony in history by getting them all married at the same time. In addition he gave them all dowries. Understandably, the mass wedding was a great success.

Tragically, Hephaistion did not live to father children. Six months after the great festival at Susa, the court moved on to the summer palace of the Persian kings at Hamadan, and to celebrate victory and to give thanks for a year without battles, Alexander arranged for another spectacular festival of games and drama, which was to last for several weeks. Some time during the festival, Hephaistion became ill with fever, and for several days was confined to bed and put on a strict diet by his doctor. After a few days he felt better, and taking advantage of the absence of his doctor, ate a meal of boiled chicken washed down with wine. It seems possible he may have had typhoid, an illness in which, though the appetite often returns before the lesions in the gut have healed, solid food causes perforation and collapse. The effect of eating was to send him into a rapid and fatal decline. Alexander was called, but arrived at the bedside too late. Hephaistion had died without him.

Alexander's grief was frantic and uncontrollable. He had the doctor crucified for negligence, and lay day and night with the body, refusing to be torn away. During this time he refused to eat or drink. His grief was a kind of madness, and no one dared to approach him. Like Achilles when Patroclus died, Alexander cut his hair and had the manes and tails of all the horses in camp shorn. It was a fortnight before he had recovered enough to order the funeral of his friend. A great stone lion was carved as a monument to Hephaistion which can still be seen at Hamadan.

Strangely, Hephaistion's death had been foretold – and so had Alexander's. Five months earlier, a deposed Persian official in Babylon had asked his brother, a prophet, to test the omens concerning his enemy, Hephaistion. A sacrifice was made and the liver examined; surprisingly, it was found to be without a lobe. The prophet sent word to his brother not to worry – Hephaistion would soon die. Now, unknown to the Persian official, the prophet sacrificed again, this time asking about Alexander, and once more the liver had no lobe. Only in crisis do prophets predict bad omens: when the official received this news he felt he must warn Alexander. Whether the warning meant anything to Alexander is not recorded, but he chose to ignore it.

There had been another prediction of death, specifying the place. Some time before, Alexander's friend, an elderly Hindu mystic called Calanus, had fallen seriously ill and decided to die, saying he had no desire to live as an invalid. He insisted on a traditional death by burning, despite Alexander's pleas. As he was mounting his pyre, Calanus made a cryptic farewell, saying he would see the king again in Babylon. After that, he allowed the flames to lap around him without flinching.

Now Alexander was determined to accord his lover funeral rites on the grandest possible scale. For this purpose he returned to Babylon, the Persian capital, which housed the royal treasuries. Already messengers had been sent to the oracle of Zeus to ask how Hephaistion should be honoured; they returned to say that he should be worshipped as a hero and a demigod. Alexander gave orders for temples in honour of Hephaistion to be built all over the empire, and decreed that his name was to be used as part of oath-taking when contracts were made.

In Babylon, the plans for the funeral pyre and the accompanying games were on an unprecedented scale. The pyre was to be 240 ft high and 200 yards square. At immense cost, it was to be constructed like a giant temple with carvings and gilded decorations.

The grandiose scheme was never carried out, because six months after Hephaistion's death, while the preparations were still being made, Alexander himself died. Stories of how this came about differ. Some said he was poisoned, others that his death was the result of heavy drinking to which he had become addicted. (Modern research has revealed that he was an alcoholic.) The Babylonian priests said that it was the fulfilment of their prophecy. But the generally accepted view is that he died of fever when weakened by a prolonged hangover. He was only thirty-two years old.

While he lay on his deathbed, his soldiers were allowed to go through his room one by one, to say goodbye to their king and general. After his death the immense empire – far too large for any one man to rule – was split up among his generals.

As we shall see in the next chapter, one of these would become the ancestor of one of the most famous queens of all time, Cleopatra of Egypt.

Chapter Three

Antony and Cleopatra

Cleopatra packed into her short life – she committed suicide at the age of thirty-nine – more experience than most women who live to be ninety.

Cleopatra was not, as most people assume, an Egyptian; her ancestry was Greek, and she was probably blonde.

Almost 300 years before her birth – in 69 BC – Alexander the Great had conquered Egypt, and founded the city of Alexandria – where Cleopatra would live and die. When Alexander caught fever and died at the age of thirty-two, one of his generals, a man named Seleucas, made himself king of Egypt, and founded a dynasty called the Ptolemies. Cleopatra dreamed of becoming the greatest of the Ptolemies, and extending her rule over the whole Mediterranean – which included Rome. In fact, she only succeeded in becoming the last of the Ptolemies.

Her grandmother was a prostitute, although she was certainly not what we would call a common streetwalker – rather a high-class courtesan whose rich clients supported her in luxury. She became the mistress of King Ptolemy, and bore him a daughter who was called Cleopatra Tryphaina. In due course, Ptolemy IX's son Ptolemy XII married his sister – as was the custom among the pharaohs who gave birth to a number of daughters, including Cleopatra and her elder sister Berenice. (It must be admitted that the sexual affairs of the pharaohs were so complicated that no historian seems to agree about precisely who gave birth to whom.)

By the time Cleopatra came into the world, the glory of

the Ptolemies was fading. Her father was nicknamed Auletes, which means the Oboe-player, and was a muddled and incompetent ruler who presided over galloping inflation. To make things worse, Rome, the greatest political force in the Mediterranean, had refused to recognize the Oboe-player's right to the throne so he was clinging to power by the skin of his teeth.

Fortunately, the Romans had their own problems. Once upon a time, Rome had been a republic, ruled by elected representatives. But three powerful men had formed an alliance, and become virtually the dictators of Rome – they were Crassus, the richest man in Rome, Pompey, one of its greatest generals, and Julius Caesar, a brilliant politician who was also known as a tireless seducer of women (and sometimes of men too).

Ancient Rome was divided into two major parties, the Conservatives and the Liberals – as modern America is divided into Republicans and Democrats, or England into Tory and Labour. Oddly enough, Caesar, Pompey and Crassus were on the side of Labour. Like most modern dictators, they realized that the support of the people could bring them far more power than the support of their political colleagues. In 59 BC, Caesar was appointed Consul of Rome and although he had a Conservative fellow Consul; he quickly became so powerful that all *his* legislation was passed, while his fellow Consul had to retreat into semi-retirement.

Towards the end of his consulate – which lasted only a year – Caesar had himself appointed governor of Gaul for the next five years. He was getting sick of Rome, with its endless backbiting and back-stabbing, and wanted an opportunity to prove himself as a soldier.

He did precisely that, conquering various rebellious tribes in Gaul, and even swooping across the Channel in 55 BC and turning Britain into a Roman colony.

Back in Rome, politics was becoming dirtier and more corrupt than ever. Crassus and Pompey ruled as fellow Consuls for a year, then Crassus decided to follow Caesar's example and go off and prove himself as a military leader. Unfortunately, he was an incompetent, and after his soldiers had been defeated, the Parthian general invited him to an amicable supper, and cut off his head. And Pompey, recognizing that Caesar was now his major rival, switched allegiance to the Conservatives.

Back in Gaul, Caesar saw the danger. But he had no desire to fight his fellow countrymen. As the end of his five years in Gaul came in sight, he sent a message to Rome suggesting that both he and Pompey should resign their positions. The Senate liked the idea, but Pompey refused. Caesar realized that if he returned to Rome with Pompey in power, his life would be short. He took the most difficult decision of his life. Although he knew that he was placing himself in the position of a criminal and a traitor, he led his army across a stream called the Rubicon, and marched into Italy.

The gamble was successful. The people of Italy wanted a popular champion, and as Caesar marched towards Rome, his army swelled with additions from every town he passed through.

Pompey could still have beaten him – he had a far more powerful army, and he had once been one of the great generals of his age. But his troops were less disciplined than Caesar's battle-hardened soldiers, and he decided to retreat and play for time. Caesar entered Rome, and although he was unarmed and alone, he became virtually dictator.

In the following year, Caesar beat Pompey's army at the battle of Pharsalus, and Pompey fled. He now made his major mistake, and decided to take refuge in Egypt. The Oboe-player – now dead – had owed him a few favours, and Pompey hoped that his son would recognize the debt.

29

True Love Stories

In fact, the new Ptolemy – Cleopatra's brother – was only a boy. But his tutors and advisers were more afraid of Caesar than of the defeated Pompey, and as Pompey landed in Egypt, he was stabbed to death by the deputation that had gone out to welcome him. When Caesar arrived shortly after, he was presented with Pompey's severed head. The Egyptian's were mildly surprised when he burst into tears and turned away in horror.

When Caesar landed in Egypt, he found it divided into two warring factions – the supporters of the boy king Ptolemy XIII, and the supporters of Cleopatra. This twenty-one-year-old girl was already a seasoned politician and schemer. When her father had died three years earlier, she and her ten-year-old brother Ptolomy had married, and become joint rulers of Egypt. But the men who really ruled Egypt were a Eunuch named Pothinus, a tutor named Theodotus, and the Captain of the King's Guard, Achillas. They expected to encounter no problems with a ten-year-old boy and an eighteen-year-old girl. They soon realized that they were mistaken – Cleopatra had a mind of her own, and the secret intention of becoming the sole ruler of Egypt. Ptolemy's counsellors plotted against her, and persuaded the people to overthrow her.

So when Caesar landed in Alexandria, hoping to gain supporters, he found himself in the middle of a political squabble. And when Pothinus found that the murder of Pompey had not gained him Caesar's support, he set about persuading the people of Alexandria that the Romans wanted to become rulers of Egypt. There were several riots in various parts of the city, and many of Caesar's soldiers were killed. Caesar became virtually a prisoner in the royal palace.

One way of resolving the situation was to bring about peace between Cleopatra and her brother. Caesar felt he had some right to tell the Egyptians what to do – Rome had put the Oboe-player back on his throne after his people had driven him into exile. (In fact, the Oboe-player's descendants still owed Rome millions of pounds.) So he ordered Ptolemy and Cleopatra to cease their quarrelling, and to reign jointly as king and queen of Egypt. Ptolemy's advisers thought they knew how to prevent this. Ptolemy was in Egypt; his sister was somewhere abroad in exile. And as long as Achillas and his army blocked the way, she could not return to Alexandria.

They underestimated Cleopatra's resourcefulness. One of her followers, a Sicilian merchant named Apollodoros, was also a dealer in carpets. Apollodoros arrived at the royal palace with a great bundle of carpets, which he claimed Caesar wanted to see, and when the carpets were unrolled in Caesar's presence, Cleopatra sat up, complaining that she had been half smothered.

It is a pity that there is no record of the scene that followed, for it was certainly one of the great romantic scenes in history. Cleopatra was not pretty, having a rather hooked nose and a large mouth, but she was intelligent, and had incomparable charm. Everyone agreed about the suppleness of her movements, and the sweetness of her voice. No doubt her charms were increased by the fact that women of the Egyptian upper classes wore nothing above the waist. And since Caesar was an incorrigible Casanova and since he had been sex-starved for a long time, his eyes must have gleamed as he told the servants to leave them alone. One historian (Jack Lindsay) speculates that before the end of that meeting, Cleopatra had lost her virginity to the Roman conqueror.

Unfortunately, the announcement that Ptolemy and Cleopatra were to become joint rulers of Egypt did not bring the expected peace. Pothinus disliked Cleopatra as much as she disliked him. So he sent a message to Achillas, telling him to recall his troops. The population of

True Love Stories

Alexandria rose up in revolt. Now Caesar was surrounded on all sides by enemies. When he learned that Pothinus was plotting to kill him, he had him assassinated. Then he sent messengers off to summon reinforcements from Syria and across the Mediterranean, then fortified the palace and the theatre next door. Since his ships in the harbour could be seized by the enemy, he had them set on fire – which also burned down the great library of Alexandria.

But Caesar was in trouble, and he knew it. At one point, he was forced to dive into the sea and swim for his life when Egyptians cut him off on the long jetty that ran out to the Pharos lighthouse. But eventually, the reinforcements arrived, and Caesar slipped through the enemy lines to join them. Then his army routed the Egyptians, and cut them down as they fled. The young King Ptolemy was drowned in the Nile.

And so Cleopatra found herself the sole ruler of Egypt, and the mistress of Rome's greatest general. For some reason, Caesar decided to spend the next nine months in Alexandria – although he was wanted in Italy. (His friend Mark Antony was acting as his deputy.) The Roman historian Suetonius claimed that Caesar was bewitched by Cleopatra, and spent the nine months in a non-stop orgy and feasting. Other historians, rejecting the idea that the great Caesar could have become the slave of a sensuous Egyptian, suggested that he remained in Alexandria until Cleopatra had borne him a son – whom she called Caesarion. Others are inclined to doubt whether Caesar was the child's father, although he himself never denied it.

At this point, Caesar realized that he had been dallying too long. Pharnaces, son of Rome's old enemy Mithridates, was trying to arouse the East to rise up against Rome. If Spain and Gaul decided to join the rebellion, it was probably the end of the Roman Empire. Caesar set out from Alexandria with three legions in 47 BC, defeated Pharnaces

Bust of Julius Caesar

at Zela, and sent a friend in Rome the reassuring message 'Veni, Vedi, Vici' – I came, I saw, I conquered.

Caesar arrived back in Rome a conquering hero, but the political situation was as unstable as ever. Pompey's son had raised a new army in Spain, and Caesar's enemies were trying to start a slave revolt to overthrow him. Caesar hardly had time to draw breath when he was forced to go out and fight again. Once again, he was triumphant. After his victory at Thapsus, he was truly the master of Rome.

Meanwhile, Cleopatra had arrived in Rome – some say that Caesar brought her back with him from Egypt. She also brought her new husband, her still younger brother Ptolemy, and her baby son Caesarion. Caesar allowed them to live on his own estate on the other side of the Tiber, and erected a statue of Cleopatra beside a statue of Venus in a new temple. Although the Romans were fairly godless, this was not the most tactful of moves. Although Caesar was married – to a lady called Calpurnia – there was a widespread belief that he was still spending most of his nights with Cleopatra, and that if he was proclaimed king – which seemed likely – he would divorce his wife and marry Cleopatra. This was one of the reasons that led to Caesar's murder only two years after he had returned to Rome, in 44 BC. The plotters were old enemies – like Cassius and Brutus – whom, with characteristic clemency, he had pardoned.

On the evening of the Ides of March, 44 BC, there was a dinner party at Caesar's home, and when someone raised the topic 'What is the best death?' Caesar replied: 'A sudden one.' The next morning, his wife begged him not to go to the Senate, saying that she had seen him in a dream covered with blood. But Brutus, whom he trusted completely, urged him to ignore this kind of superstition. When Caesar entered and sat down, the conspirators flung themselves on him and stabbed him to death. When he saw Brutus raising his knife, he is reported to have said: 'You too, my son?' and pulled his robe over his face, allowing the conspirators to stab him again and again.

The sequel is known to every schoolchild who has read Shakespeare's *Julius Caesar*. Caesar's friend Mark Antony – who had been deliberately detained in conversation while Caesar was murdered – managed to get hold of Caesar's will, and saw that Caesar had left his gardens to the people of Rome as a public park, and had left a small legacy to every citizen – about £25. Rumours of the will soon spread throughout Rome. And when Antony gave the funeral oration besides Caesar's corpse, his indignation boiled over, and members of the crowd began to sob and throw things on the funeral pyre as offerings – women threw their jewels, musicians threw their instruments, soldiers threw their swords. The riots in Rome lasted for three days, and several of the conspirators were killed – although Brutus and Cassius were not among them. Antony finally had to restore order with his own soldiers.

After Caesar's death, Cleopatra lost no time in returning to Alexandria. And at about this time, her younger brother – and consort – seems to have vanished from the scene. No one is quite sure how this happened, although the historian Josephus states that she poisoned the boy. That seems highly likely. She had only accepted him as her consort because Caesar insisted, and now Caesar was dead, she wanted to reign alone.

In Rome, Antony had quickly become rich and powerful – so much so that the Senate sent off for Caesar's adopted son, Octavius, who was serving with the army abroad. He was horrified to hear of Caesar's murder, and shocked at the ingratitude of Rome towards its benefactor. He was also shocked when he returned to Rome, and discovered that Antony had failed to give the common people their legacy due under Caesar's will. Octavius borrowed the money himself from Caesar's friends and distributed it. Antony was furious, and suspected that Octavius was planning to have him assassinated. The two of them quarrelled, and there was a battle between their armies at Mutina, which Antony lost. But when Octavius got back to Rome, and realized that Caesar's enemies were still plotting against him, he decided that it might be better to forgive Antony and accept his friendship. Their combined armies marched on Rome, and took it without resistance. There followed one of the worst reigns of terror in Rome's history, and hundreds were murdered.

Brutus and Cassius had fled. They raised money by a campaign of terror in the cities of the East, and used it to finance their campaign. But it was all to no purpose. Two years after Caesar's assassination, the two armies met at Philippi. Brutus and Cassius lost, and both committed suicide.

Now although Antony and Octavius were partners, Antony regarded himself as Caesar's true successor. After all, Octavius was little more than a boy, and moreover, he was in poor health. When the victors divided the spoils, Antony took Egypt, Greece and the East, Octavius took the West, including Europe, and Lepidus, the third member of the partnership, took Africa. Antony went off to Ephesus – in Greece – raised vast sums in taxes, and threw himself into an orgy of sensuality. His appetite for sex was gargantuan, and he used his position as the ruler of Greece to sleep with every woman – married or unmarried – who took his fancy.

Who was this Mark Antony, who had suddenly become the master of a third of the civilized world? Fourteen years older than Cleopatra, he was the son of a man who had squandered the family fortune, and who was killed while attacking Crete. After the death of his father, Antony was brought up by a stepfather who was executed in one of Rome's endless political squabbles. As a young man,

Antony borrowed large sums of money, ran up huge debts, and was forced to fly from his creditors to Greece, where he became a cavalry officer. A big man with the strength of a bull, he made a magnificent soldier.

It was while serving under Caesar in Gaul that he began his slow ascent to power. Caesar liked the vigorous young officer who obviously admired him to the point of adoration. He sent him back to Rome, and arranged for him to take the first steps on the political ladder. But Anthony soon found himself up against Caesar's enemies. When the Senate voted to deprive Caesar of his command, Antony hurried back to Gaul, and was at Caesar's side when he crossed the Rubicon. Then, when Caesar was master of Italy, and went off to pacify Spain, Mark Antony remained behind as Caesar's representative. When Caesar came back from Egypt, and went off to fight in Africa, Mark Antony was once again the deputy ruler in Italy.

Like Caesar, he was loved by his troops. Unlike Caesar, he had no real desire for power – except as a means of living the kind of life he enjoyed.

And it was while he was enjoying life in Tarsus that he decided to send for Cleopatra. It was the beginning of one of the most famous love affairs in history.

Why did he send for Cleopatra? It is possible that he had been hoping to seduce her for years. Mark Antony had been the young officer who, at the age of twenty-seven, had restored the throne to her father, the Oboe-player. Admittedly, he was under the orders of a man called Aulus Gabinius, who was Proconsul of Syria, and who, in turn, was under the orders of Pompey. But it was Mark Antony who led the way to Alexandria at the head of an army and expelled the Oboe-player's enemies. The Oboe-player lost no time in executing his daughter Berenice, Cleopatra's elder sister, so making Cleopatra the heir to the throne.

Cleopatra was only thirteen at the time, but she was

already vivacious and strong-minded. There can be little doubt that she attracted the attention of the young Roman cavalry officer who regarded all women as his natural prey. But Antony had to return to Rome, and it was Julius Caesar who – eight years later – made her his mistress.

So it seems more than likely that, when Antony summoned her to Tarsus – on some feeble accusation that she had raised taxes for Brutus and Cassius – he was simply making up for lost time. And it is highly likely that, when Cleopatra set out from Alexandria, she guessed precisely what he had in mind.

Shakespeare has made the scene of their meeting famous – the enormous barge 'like a burnished throne', with purple sails and silver oars, gliding up the river Cydnus to the music of harps and flutes. The decks were full of servant girls dressed as sea nymphs, and boys like Cupids. The smell of rich perfumes and incenses wafted across the water. Cleopatra herself dressed as Venus, lay under a canopy made of gold cloth. Antony sat waiting for her on a golden throne, but by the time she arrived, he had been deserted – everyone had rushed off to watch her arrival.

He invited her to supper; she said she would prefer for him to come and have supper on board with her. She took care to impress him with her extravagance and splendour, even creating a kind of light-show in which hundreds of rush-lights were arranged in patterns of rectangles and circles.

The next day, Antony was Cleopatra's host to dinner and he had the humour to make fun of the simplicity of his own arrangements compared to hers.

They liked one another immediately. Antony was bluff, good-natured, and he had a soldier's taste for crude jokes. Cleopatra was the kind of highly dominant woman who enjoyed crude jokes, and the two of them were soon exchanging pleasantries like old comrades.

On the third and fourth day, Cleopatra was once again the hostess, and she set out deliberately to surpass herself. She spent over a thousand pounds on roses, and had them spread all over the dining room to a depth of two feet, and hung in nets from the ceiling. All the silver and gold dishes were presented to Antony as presents. Antony's officers were given couches on which they had lain, as well as the expensive cloths that covered them – Cleopatra provided slaves to carry them back to their barracks.

There can be no doubt that it was Antony who was ensnared. Cleopatra was undoubtedly his intellectual superior. She spoke a dozen languages, and was familiar with poetry, philosophy and art. By comparison, he must have felt himself a crude soldier. Although intelligent, he was no intellectual. Cleopatra was not only beautiful and sophisticated; she possessed a mind that had fascinated Julius Caesar. But she was the Queen of Egypt and he was the King of Egypt – as well as of Greece and Syria. How soon they became lovers is not clear. She probably realized that surrendering too quickly would be counter-productive. Antony was a typical soldier; once he had possessed a woman, he began to lose interest. Cleopatra had already made him wait for nearly a year before she obeyed his summons to Tarsus. Now she probably made him wait still further, returning to Alexandria, and inviting him to come and spend the winter there.

When Antony arrived in Alexandria, he realized why Cleopatra was so eager to cling to power. Rome was a democracy, and although men could be murdered with impunity, its citizens were still – in theory – equal. In Egypt, Cleopatra was absolute ruler. She had thousands of servants, all of whom regarded her as a goddess. Her generosity and her extravagance were equally amazing. She could have a man executed by merely raising her eyebrows, but she could also make him a millionaire by snapping her fingers at her treasurer. For Cleopatra, power was synonymous with being completely alive.

In Alexandria, life turned into a non-stop party. She ate with him, drank with him, slept with him, played dice with him, went hunting and fishing with him, joined in his practical jokes, even dressed up as a servant-girl and went slumming with him. One historian describes how his grandfather was allowed to look into the royal kitchen when supper was being prepared, and saw eight wild boars roasting on spits, as well as tables laden with every other kind of food. When he asked how many guests were coming to supper, the cook laughed and explained that there were only about a dozen. But since Antony enjoyed talking as much as eating and drinking, and since hot food spoiled in the meantime, they cooked half a dozen suppers, one after the other, to make sure that the food was always perfect.

Unfortunately, the feasting had to stop. In the following spring, the Parthians invaded the Roman provinces in Asia Minor, and Antony had to hurry back to the wars. It was another three years before Cleopatra saw him again; meanwhile, she bore him twins. Antony was forced to hurry from Asia Minor back to Rome. His wife Fulvia and his brother Lucius were doing their best to overthrow Octavius. Rome was in chaos. Pompey's son Sextus was blockading the import of food. Unemployment was high, and taxation had ruined all but the very rich. Fulvia, who was as dominant as Cleopatra, saw an opportunity of seizing power for herself and her husband, and raised an army. Octavius's general besieged Lucius in Perusia and forced him to surrender. Antony tried to come to his brother's rescue, and besieged Octavius's troops in Brundisiam. The two armies refused to fight, and Antony and Octavius again shook hands. When Fulvia died, Antony married Octavius's sister Octavia, and then joined Octavius in destroying the fleet of Pompey's son.

Antony and Cleopatra

Unlike some of Antony's women, Octavia was beautiful, gentle and good. They went together to Athens, where Antony attended the classes of philosophers. But the academic life bored him, and he was soon brooding on how to make a permanent conquest of Parthia – a country that corresponded roughly to modern Iraq. The problem was that such an expedition would require vast sums of money. The only person he knew who possessed vast sums of money was Cleopatra. So he sent Octavia back to Rome, and asked Cleopatra to meet him in Antioch.

The moment he saw her again, he knew that his marriage to Octavia had been a mistake. Cleopatra was equally determined not to lose him again. Probably at her suggestion, he sent an annulment of his marriage to Octavia in Rome, and then did the rashest thing he had done in his whole life, and married Cleopatra. It was like a deliberate insult to Octavius – not to mention his fellow citizens in Rome. The marriage was not even valid in Roman law. In a single stroke, he had made himself more enemies than he had made in the whole of his life.

Antony didn't care. He was the new pharaoh of Egypt, and Cleopatra sat beside him on the throne. Their twins were heirs to the throne. And since Antony also regarded himself as the ruler of various Roman provinces – like Crete, Cyprus, Cilicia (in Turkey), Judaea, Arabia and Phoenicia – he handed over most of these to Cleopatra as a wedding present. She even persuaded him to give her large portions of Syria, Lebanon and the Balsam Groves of Jericho in Judaea – which actually belonged to King Herod, who ruled it on behalf of Rome. It is said that during Antony's long absence, she had tried to seduce Herod when he was on his way through Egypt, and was furious with him for declining to share her bed. Now, as she took a tour of her new domains, Herod smiled amiably and pretended to be delighted to see her, while he secretly dreamed of revenge.

Antony now had all the money he wanted for his Parthian campaign, and set off with his army to prove himself as great a general as Julius Caesar. The whole campaign was a disaster. He failed to subdue the Parthian citadels, and then, as winter came on, was forced to retreat, losing nearly half his 100,000 men in the bleak and hostile territory. He soothed his wounded pride by annexing Armenia, and when he got back to Alexandria, granted himself a triumph. Antony and Cleopatra sat side by side on a golden throne, with their own three children – Cleopatra had given birth again – and little Caesarion, beside them. Antony caused further offence to Octavius by declaring Caesarion to be Caesar's heir, which meant, in effect, that Octavius was a usurper. Cleopatra was given the title of Queen of Kings, and Caesarion King of Kings. The other children were made kings of various territories in Antony's 'empire'. Octavius aroused the Roman people to fury by telling them that Antony was giving away large parts of the Roman Empire to a foreigner, and that he intended to transfer the capital of the Roman Empire to Alexandria. The Roman Senate deprived Antony of his office of Consul. Octavius's argument was that Cleopatra was scheming to become Queen of the Roman Empire – and he was probably not far from the truth.

A clash between Antony and Octavius was inevitable. In 32 BC, Octavius declared war against Cleopatra – which made it sound like a patriotic war for the independence of Italy rather than a squabble between two powerful Romans.

With Cleopatra's money – and her navy – behind him, Antony was untroubled. That September, he moved 500 warships to the west coast of Greece, as well as 100,000 infantrymen and 12,000 cavalry. He suffered an immediate setback when Octavius's admiral Agrippa captured a number of Greek naval bases and cut off their supply routes to Egypt. Meanwhile, Octavius moved into northern Greece with his cavalry, infantry and ships. He was vastly outnumbered by Antony's forces, but his ships were more manoeuvrable, and Antony's army was short of supplies because of the blockade. This was the point where the support of Herod might have made a crucial difference – but Herod, understandably, was delighted to see Cleopatra stewing in her own juice.

The confrontation finally took place at Actium on 2 September, 31 BC. Antony probably made his greatest mistake in deciding to risk everything on a naval battle probably because his ships outnumbered the enemy by about eighty. He made the same mistake that the Spanish Armada was to make almost seventeen centuries later. His huge ships were too clumsy for a sea battle that depended on speed. Antony and his admirals Marcus Octavius and Sosius sailed out to meet the three enemy squadrons, while Cleopatra waited with her squadron in the rear. Halfway through the day, it was obvious that the lighter vessels of Octavius – with two banks of oars – had the advantage. Finally, Antony's squadron – on the northern flank – began to give way. This was the point where Cleopatra should have come to his aid. Instead, she sailed between the two fleets, and turned back towards Egypt. Instead of trying to rally his forces, Antony transferred to a faster vessel and followed her. His leaderless fleet was doomed. The lighter vessels of Octavius sailed between the ships and set fire to them by throwing burning brands on board. At the end of the day, Antony's fleet surrendered. Five thousand of his men were dead.

Antony caught up with Cleopatra, and went on board her ship. But he was so furious that he refused to speak to her for three days. Then they made up, and decided that, if they could not live together, at least they could die together.

Cleopatra

In fact, they had a breathing space. Octavius had to go back to Italy to quell a mutiny among his troops, then to Asia, to punish the rulers who had supported Antony against him, and only then to Alexandria.

In his last days, Antony, in a state of numb despair, became a kind of hermit, retiring to an island near the Pharos. It was Cleopatra who had to make all the preparations to defend Alexandria, and to attempt to rally forces that had no desire to share in her destruction. She even tried to save her navy by having the ships dragged on huge wooden wheels across the narrow isthmus of land to the Red Sea. Marauding Arabs destroyed them.

As Octavius approached, Antony wrote to him reminding him of their past friendship, and promising to kill himself if he would spare Cleopatra. Octavius did not deign to reply. He also ignored a message from Cleopatra agreeing to surrender. Cleopatra locked herself in a magnificent mausoleum that had been specially built for her, together with all her treasure, and threatened Octavius that she would destroy it all unless he granted an honourable peace. Antony, meanwhile, roused himself to a last tremendous effort, and for a while, it even looked as if he was gaining the upper hand. The next day, as he saw Cleopatra's soldiers surrender, and heard a report that she had committed suicide, he seized his sword and stabbed himself. Soon after that, he heard the news that she was still alive, and asked to be taken to the mausoleum. He was drawn up through an upper window, and he drank some wine. Then he began to bleed to death, and died in Cleopatra's arms.

Octavius marched into Alexandria. He allowed Cleopatra to bury her lover, then told her that he intended to take her back to Rome with him. She knew what that meant – that she would be led through the streets to grace Octavius's triumph. When she appeared to accept this, Octavius allowed her to go.

True Love Stories

A few days before she was due to leave for Rome, a peasant came to her door with a basket of figs. The guard nodded and let him pass.

Dressed in her royal robes, Cleopatra pushed back the figs, and took out the asp that was hidden underneath them. The bite of this tiny snake was deadly. She wrote a last note to Octavius, telling him that it was impossible for her to surrender, and when the servant had gone, pressed the asp against her breast.

When one of Octavius's officers rushed into the room, Cleopatra was already dead. She was thirty-nine, and had been a queen for twenty-two years. Her ambition and lack of self-control had led to the destruction of her country. After the death of Cleopatra, Egypt became a Roman province.

King Arthur and Queen Guinevere

Most present-day historians accept that King Arthur was in reality a great leader of the British against the incursions of the Anglo-Saxons into the British Isles. By his leadership and skill in uniting the tribes under his command and winning a great battle, he held back the tide of invasion for a fifty-year period of relative peace.

But all the legends about him speak of his beautiful wife Guinevere and also of her seduction by Lancelot, one of Arthur's knights of the Round Table.

Is there any proof that these two characters did exist and the romantic triangle also? Well it seems certain that Lancelot was purely an invention of the troubadours of the Middle Ages who felt obliged to invent him for their recitals of the Arthurian tales. They had to cater for that period's fascination with adulterous love and to satisfy the requests of the aristocratic French ladies who employed them. On the other hand, the real existence of Queen Guinevere and her marriage to Arthur seems to be at least a possibility.

For on an April day in 1191 the monks of Glastonbury Abbey started on a deep excavation in a particular spot between two tall stone crosses that had stood in their ancient burial ground for as long as anyone could remember. King Henry II had requested this investigation because of a persistent story that an important person of rank, perhaps even King Arthur himself, had once been buried there.

Now a chronicler, Ralph of Coggeshall, who visited the abbey the next day set down for posterity what the monks actually found, and what he had to say then was corroborated in the following year by another writer, Giraldus, and also by a monk who subsequently wrote a long history of his abbey.

They all recorded that after digging down for about nine feet, much deeper than the level of the usual grave, the monks came across a large stone embedded in the ground. Laid underneath it face down was a leaden cross inscribed in Latin in early lettering – 'Here lies the great King Arthur, in the isle of Avalon buried'. The second chronicler Giraldus says that the cross also had inscribed on it – 'with Guinevere, his second wife'.

Greatly encouraged, the monks persisted with their digging and when their excavations had reached the dangerous depth of fifteen feet in the black burial ground soil, they uncovered the skeleton of a man who had been of extraordinary height, laid with his skull facing to the East, the sign of a Christian burial of an earlier time. Mingled with bones of this skeleton were the bones of a much smaller person, and clinging to one of these was a tress of red gold hair that still gleamed in the dim light.

The monks were certain that they had found the grave of King Arthur and of Queen Guinevere. Reaching down in excitement one of the monks leant to touch the hair and the chronicler records that he tumbled into the grave. Unfortunately, the vibration of his fall and the air penetrating into the grave caused the golden hair to crumble away to dust. The bones remained intact, and were subsequently reinterred with great ceremony in two magnificent shrines placed before the high altar of the new abbey church. In this way the tombs of Arthur and Guinevere became a focus of pilgrimage throughout the Middle Ages until at last they were destroyed in the Reformation. The leaden cross survived to be examined and described again by a historian in the sixteenth century.

After that it disappeared and has yet to be found again. But the accounts of what the monks found on that April day do seem to show that Arthur and Guinevere and their loving relationship in life were not just an invention of the troubadours.

Chapter Four

Abelard and Heloise

Peter Abelard was one of the most influential thinkers of his time. A man of tremendous charisma, he was adored by his students, who regarded him as the world's greatest philosopher. Abelard himself was not entirely opposed to this opinion, and would certainly have been saddened to learn that he is remembered mainly as the lover of the beautiful Heloise.

Abelard was born at Pallet, in Brittany, the son of a knight. In those days, a knight meant literally someone who devoted his life to wars and fighting, but Abelard had an instinctive contempt for the military mentality. He had a deep and powerful compulsion to make use of his mind. So he turned his back on a career in the army, sacrificed his inheritance, and went to Paris to study philosophy.

Now before we can get on with the love story, we need to understand why Abelard became one of the most influential – and controversial – thinkers of his age, which in turn requires understanding something about the quarrels of medieval philosophers. As far as the Middle Ages were concerned, there were only two great philosophers: Plato and Aristotle. Plato believed that there is a kind of mystical reality behind this messy, accidental world of everyday life. His pupil Aristotle was more down to earth. He had a scientific turn of mind, and believed in looking at the world with the eye of a practical man.

Now in the Middle Ages, the Catholic Church claimed to have a total monopoly on truth. Jesus had come down to earth to save the world from the consequences of the sin of

True Love Stories

Adam, and that was the only thing worth knowing. But since Plato believed in a 'higher reality', he could be regarded as the predecessor of Christian teaching. And since Aristotle had done his best to explain the whole world in practical terms, his philosophy could be regarded as a reason why the good Christian did not have to think for himself.

But there was an obvious problem. Even to read Plato and Aristotle meant that a man had to exercise his intelligence. Was this not in itself a contradiction of the Church's teaching that all a man needed to get to heaven was faith in the Holy Trinity? But whether the Church liked it or not, intelligent people felt the need to use their heads, and so philosophers continued to argue about which was the most important: faith or reason. Of course, if any philosopher had dared to state flatly that reason was more important than faith, he would probably have been burned at the stake. So instead, philosophers argued about whether Plato or Aristotle was the greater thinker.

As soon as he arrived in Paris, Abelard found himself embroiled in this controversy. He became a pupil of a teacher named Roscellin, who had no patience with the followers of Plato (known as Platonists). They believed that this everyday world is just a crude reflection of a higher world of ideas or 'forms'. For example, the world is full of round things, from the sun and moon to oranges and coins. According to Plato, *all* round things are just crude versions of an idea or 'form' called roundness. And this form exists in a world of its own, together with such qualities as blueness, bitterness and goodness. If a carpenter wants to make a table, he must have the *idea* of a table in his mind before he begins to make it. So, in a sense, the idea of a table is more important than the real table.

Roscellin disagreed. He quite rightly thought that the idea of a ghostly world of 'forms', like some timeless

Peter Abelard

museum situated in a kind of fifth dimension, was an absurdity. He insisted that roundness is only a reality because it is attached to objects like coins and oranges.

Abelard was inclined to agree with him. But he was also open-minded enough to become a student of one of Roscellin's ex-pupils, William of Champeaux, who had come to reject Roscellin's teaching. For a while, Abelard found William of Champeaux's Platonism exciting; but then gradually came to reject it. It seemed to him that there was something wrong with both his teachers. Roscellin was too down-to-earth, and William of Champeaux was too up-in-the-air.

And so, driven out of Paris by the opposition of William of Champeaux, he set up his own school at Melun a few miles away. There he continued his battle against William of Champeaux so effectively that William finally admitted defeat, and most of his pupils left him and flocked to Abelard.

Abelard's solution of the problem was typical of his common sense. He could see that Plato's ghostly museum is an absurdity, but he could also see that it is absurd to say that there is no such thing as roundness apart from round objects. Roundness is a mathematical shape, and it would exist whether there are any round objects or not. In other words, roundness is a *logical idea* which exists apart from any round object, but at the same time is not a museum piece in a phantom world of 'forms'.

Abelard was, in effect, a kind of philosophical pop star. His pupils admired his manner as much as the things he said. They all did their best to imitate him. In AD 1115, by the time he was in his mid-thirties, Abelard was one of the best known philosophers in Europe. Pupils travelled from all over the civilized world to listen to him.

And it was at this point that he fell in love with one of his pupils, Heloise. She was only seventeen when he first met her – twenty years his junior. But she was intelligent as well as beautiful, and known for her learning. Her parents had died when she was a baby, and she was brought up by her uncle, Canon Fulbert, who was at Notre Dame.

Whether Abelard was really in love with her, or whether he was simply unable to resist a beautiful girl who regarded him as a father figure, will never be known. He probably felt that he deserved some worldly pleasure in compensation for the enormous intellectual energy that he hurled into combating his opponents. For someone who had led a celibate life – for, like every other teacher of his age, Abelard was also a priest – a beautiful seventeen-year-old who regarded him with the same adoration as the rest of his students was probably irresistible.

The best account of their affair is contained in Helen Waddell's novel *Peter Abelard*, which is based on Abelard's own autobiography, *The Story of my Calamities*.

There can be no doubt that it was Abelard who seduced Heloise, and that he found it easy to do. To begin with, both he and Heloise were living in the house of her uncle, Canon Fulbert. *Peter Abelard* describes how, for night after night, he had kissed her repeatedly, and had then held her on the threshold of her room, kissing her again and again. Then, after several nights, he had leaned close to her and murmured, 'Tomorrow night.' Faced with the idea of descending into the sins of the flesh, Heloise was suddenly terrified. Would she wake up in the morning feeling foul and depraved?

Early the next morning, she had heard him shouting to his servant Guibert to bring him one of his books of theology. Heloise got out of bed; and, with only her cloak wrapped around her, went to help him find it. But as Abelard came up the staircase, and saw her standing at the top with the short cloak hanging loosely around her, he stared at her with such obvious sexual desire that she was shaken.

Suddenly unable to face the thought of yielding her

virginity, she seized the opportunity of spending the day at the convent of Argenteuil, whose Abbess was the cousin of Gilles de Vannes, the Canon of Notre Dame and one of Abelard's closest friends. Gilles told her that she could ride pillion behind his servant Jehan who was taking an offering to the Abbess.

When Abelard came back and found that Heloise had gone, he was at first terrified that she had decided to confess her 'sin' to the Abbess of Argenteuil. He also suspected that Canon Fulbert had realized what was going on, and had sent Heloise away. But when he talked to the Canon, it seemed obvious that the old man was unsuspicious. Unable to sit still, Abelard walked out into the night, and when he returned, emotionally and physically exhausted, in the early hours of the morning, he found Heloise waiting for him in his room. His weariness touched her heart, and she cradled his head against her breast. In his relief at seeing her again, the question of making her his mistress was forgotten.

But a few nights later, shortly after Easter, he went quietly into her room to stare at her as she lay asleep. He was unable to resist touching her, and she woke up. He looked so pale that she thought he must have a fever. He told her that he had suddenly been gripped by the fear that he was about to lose her. This time, she yielded to his kisses, and allowed him into her bed.

In the early hours of the morning, they heard unsteady footsteps mounting the stair. Then her door opened, and Canon Fulbert came in, holding a candle. When he saw them in bed together, he gave a strange cry, and collapsed on the floor. Fulbert had had a mild stroke.

Abelard moved out of his house. Canon Fulbert was furious, but believed that, now the lovers were separated, the affair was over. Helen Waddell seems to suspect that Fulbert entertained some kind of incestuous passion for his niece. Or it may have been simply that he adored her like a daughter, and felt that he had been betrayed. Now he seemed to veer between hatred and flashes of his old tenderness. On one occasion, he even struck her.

A few months later, Heloise discovered that she was pregnant. Abelard was shattered – not because of the disgrace, but because of the position he had put her in. He decided to take her away to the house of his sister in Brittany. There they could spend the summer together, and she could have the baby.

Fulbert's reaction was to sink into a kind of nervous depression. It was the opinion of Gilles de Vannes that he became insane. Stricken by conscience, Abelard waited for him one evening when he was returning to his own house, and asked him if he could have Heloise's hand in marriage. Delighted and relieved, the old man said yes.

Yet when Abelard joined Heloise in Brittany, he was surprised at her resistance. She realized that marriage could destroy his career. He told her that Fulbert had promised to keep the marriage a secret. But Heloise was quite certain that her uncle would not keep his promise. Finally, with deep misgivings, she agreed. Their baby proved to be a son, whom they called Astrolabius.

The following Easter, they left the child with Abelard's sister, and Heloise, dressed in boy's clothes, returned with him to Paris. There she moved back into the house of her uncle.

But she proved to be correct; Fulbert was unable to keep a secret. One day, in front of two distinguished visitors – Geoffrey of Chartres and Alberic of Rheims – he suddenly declared that he was proud of his niece because she was married to a great man – Peter Abelard. The two clerics looked bewildered, and then offered Fulbert and Heloise their congratulations. Heloise replied coolly: 'My uncle is mistaken. I am not married to Master Peter.'

Alberic asked: 'Then you are not his wife?'

Heloise shook her head. 'No, I am his mistress.'

As she said this, Fulbert began to shriek and grabbed her by the throat. Then, before the other two could pull him off, he collapsed on the floor with another stroke.

To avoid scandal, Heloise moved to the convent of Argenteuil. Abelard remained in Paris, still living in the house of Canon Fulbert. But he made sure that his servant kept the door locked at night.

The old man now seemed madder than before. He tried to bribe Abelard's servant with a hundred gold pieces – an enormous sum of money – to slip a sleeping powder into his master's drink, and then leave his door unlocked. The servant took the money, but when it came to it, was unable to drop the powder into the posset – milk curdled with wine – that Abelard always drank before going to bed. But he left his master's door unlocked.

That night, Fulbert led three hired ruffians into Abelard's room. Two of them held him down while the third castrated him.

The servant, drunk and suddenly tormented by his conscience, told two of Abelard's pupils what he had done. They rushed back to the house, but it was too late. Abelard was writhing in agony on the bloodstained bed.

This was, in effect, the end of the love affair. Abelard decided to become a monk at St Denis. Heloise, against her will, allowed herself to be persuaded to become a nun in the convent at Argenteuil.

It was by no means the end of Abelard's life. He was castrated at the age of thirty-nine, and still had another twenty-four years to live. They were filled with controversy and bitterness; Abelard seemed to enjoy making enemies. Even at the Abbey of St Denis he antagonized his fellow monks by criticizing their way of life. He made a collection of texts from the Bible designed to show inconsistencies in

Christian teaching. It was called *Sic et non (Yes and No)* and
was to cause him a great deal of trouble. The purpose was
not basically to discredit Christian teaching, but to try to
teach students the way that words change their meanings in
different contexts, and over the course of centuries. (It is
this preoccupation with language that makes Abelard so
sympathetic to modern philosophers.) He landed himself in
even deeper trouble with a book about the Holy Trinity,
which was condemned as heretical. Here his chief opponent
was Bernard of Clairvaux – later Saint Bernard – who hated
Abelard's whole intellectual approach to religion and
philosophy. The followers of Abelard became known as
Nominalists, which meant that they believed that abstract
ideas – like roundness – were merely words (or names.) The
opposing school, which believed (like Plato) that ideas
formed a kind of ultimate reality, became known as
Realists. In 1121, a council held at Soissons, inspired by
Bernard of Clairvaux, condemned Abelard as a heretic. For
a while, he was under house arrest in the Abbey of Saint-
Medard. Back at the Abbey of St Denis, he quarrelled so
violently with the monks that they threatened to bring him
to trial before the King of France. He had to flee, and found
asylum with Count Theobald of Champagne. There he did
his best to become a hermit, but was pursued by enthusiastic students who persuaded him to return to teaching. In
1125, he became abbot of a remote monastery in Brittany,
but again, his combative – and now rather irritable – spirit
caused great offence and attempts were actually made to
kill him. After ten miserable years, he left.

Eventually, Abelard and Heloise were to come together
again – but not as lovers. When Abelard had attempted to
become a hermit, he had retreated to a desert place near
Nogent-sur-Seine, and his students had built him an
oratory which he called the Paraclete. When the convent at
Argenteuil broke up, Abelard established Heloise as the

True Love Stories

head of a new convent in the now deserted Paraclete. It was after his flight from the monastery in Brittany that he wrote his famous *Historia Calamitatum* (*History of my Calamities*) which led Heloise to write him three love letters. Abelard wrote her four letters, and these seven are among the most famous love letters in the world.

The last years of Abelard's life were embittered by the long-standing quarrel with Bernard of Clairvaux. In 1141, a council at Sens charged him with heresy again. As Bernard was about to open the case against him, Abelard decided to appeal directly to the Pope. It made no difference; Abelard was condemned at Sens, and in the following year, this was confirmed by Pope Innocent II. Now a broken man, Abelard set out for Rome to make a direct personal plea, but collapsed with exhaustion at the Abbey of Cluny, where he was protected by the abbot, Peter the Venerable. Peter succeeded in reconciling him with Bernard of Clairvaux, but Abelard was too tired to return to teaching. For the remaining months of his life, he lived as a Cluniac monk, and died in the Abbey on 21 April 1142. His body was sent back to Heloise at the Paraclete. Heloise lived another twenty-two years, until 1164. Now, their ashes lie in the same tomb in the cemetery of Père Lachaise in Paris.

Chapter Five

Taj Mahal

One Victorian Englishwoman was so entranced by the Taj Mahal that she exclaimed: 'I feel that I would like to die tomorrow if my bones were to be covered by such a monument.'

It was built between 1630 and 1648 by the Moghul Emperor Shah Jahan, in memory of his wife Mumtaz (shortened to Taj) Mahal. But it was this same Shah Jahan, the builder of India's most beautiful shrine, who started a tradition of assassinating relatives that finally led to the downfall of the Moghul dynasty.

Shah Jahan was the son of the Emperor Jahangir, who came to the throne in 1605. Jahangir was a civilized man who loved art and philosophy. He was also, like so many of the Moghuls, an opium addict and an alcoholic – both his brothers had died of alcoholism. He describes in his diary how, from the first cup of sweet yellow wine at seventeen, he quickly began to drink so much that wine ceased to affect him, so he went on to arrack (roughly the same strength as whisky) drinking up to twenty cups per day. When his doctor warned him that he would be dead in six months if he continued, he cut down to six cups of wine mixed with arrack. And since this was inadequate, he added large quantities of opium. All of which may explain why, although usually a gentle man, he could explode into outbursts of manic cruelty. One of his pleasures was to watch condemned men trampled to death by elephants under his balcony.

Like most of the Moghuls, the young Jahangir was

True Love Stories

sexually insatiable, and had a harem of 300 or so concubines. (A Moslem was allowed only four wives, but an indefinite number of mistresses.) When alcohol and opium destroyed the Emperor's interest in sex, the concubines found the confinement of the harem appallingly dull – an English doctor tells how the women would occasionally pretend to be ill, merely so they could request a visit from the doctor and have some conversation. He also tells how the patient would thrust the part requiring attention – an arm or a leg – out from behind a curtain for him to examine. Sometimes, when he passed his hand through the aperture to feel her temperature, the lady would bite his fingers, or even place his hand on her naked breast. Since he was being carefully watched by eunuchs, he had to make an effort to show no sign of what was happening. The same doctor added that the eunuchs made sure that no cucumbers or similar vegetables were allowed into the harem.

The eunuchs, although sterile, were by no means impotent, and there seem to have been many examples of bored concubines amusing themselves with their gaolers – a dangerous practice, since detection would involve a painful death for both.

Jahangir was lucky in his choice of his main wife, the daughter of a penniless Persian who came to India seeking his fortune, and rose to a rank corresponding to Grand Vizier. The girl was first married to one of Jahangir's officers, but was left a widow at the age of thirty. Jahangir met her at a kind of mock-bazaar set up by his courtiers and their wives for the royal amusement (it enabled them to flirt and play at being commoners), and immediately fell in love with her. He married her, and bestowed on her the name Nur Mahal, meaning Light of the Palace. She was a poet, artist, dress designer and even a keen hunter (shooting tigers from a howdah on top of an elephant). She became empress, and her family was soon the most influential in the land. Her brother Asaf Khan became a kind of deputy Grand Vizier. The British ambassador – who was in India trying to persuade the Emperor to make concessions on behalf of the East India Company – wrote to Prince Charles (the future Charles the First) that the King's wife 'governs him and winds him up at her pleasure' (implying he was a clockwork toy).

Now Jahangir had four sons. The eldest, Khusrau, should have been the heir to the throne – except that the Moghuls preferred to make their own choice about who was fit to succeed them. The next, Parwiz, was an alcoholic, and would eventually die of drink. It was the third, Prince Khurran, who was Jahangir's favourite, and who would, in due course, call himself Shah Jahan. (To avoid confusion we shall follow his example.) The fourth, Prince Shahriyar, was the son of a concubine, and was lacklustre and feeble.

The Empress set about consolidating her position by marrying the daughter of her first marriage to Prince Shahriyar – just in case, by some fluke, he came to the throne. The daughter of her brother, the deputy Grand Vizier, was married off to Shah Jahan, in an arranged marriage, when he was twenty. Her real name was Arjumand Banu, but Shah Jahan called her Mumtaz Mahal, meaning the Light of the Palace. Since it was to her that her husband would build the Taj Mahal, we shall refer to her as Taj, an abbreviation of Mumtaz.

Now in royal marriages it was common for the husband and wife to meet for the first time at the wedding, the primary purpose being to join two powerful families. The question of whether or not the couple liked one another was largely irrelevant. Fortunately, the prince who would become Shah Jahan fell as completely in love with Taj as his father had with Nur Mahal.

There was one basic difference. The Empress had

Mumtaz-i-Mahal, for whom Shah Jahan built the Taj Mahal

virtually taken over the government of the country, ruling
it from the harem. Taj was an altogether softer and gentler
character, who confined herself to giving her husband love,
support and advice. He proved his passion by begetting
upon her fourteen children in nineteen years, of whom only
seven survived. Yet in spite of being almost permanently
pregnant, she proved to be the ideal wife and helpmate for
a Moghul emperor.

Except, of course, that at this stage Shah Jahan was still a
long way from being emperor. His elder brother Khusrau
had his eye on the throne, and his father kept him at court,

where he could prevent him from getting into mischief. Khusrau soon grew bored with court life. And since the future Shah Jahan was obviously his father's favourite, he felt that it was time to assert his independence. On the pretence of visiting the great Akbar's tomb, he escaped from court, and began to raise an army. With this he proceeded to besiege Lahore. Jahangir's army arrived, and Khusrau's inexperienced soldiers were easily defeated. Khusrau and two companions tried to row across the river, but their boat became stuck in the shallows, and they had to sit there until they were captured, and dragged in front of Jahangir in his garden. The Emperor was merciful to his son, but subjected the two companions to a highly unpleasant ordeal. Each was sewn inside the skin of a newly slaughtered animal – one an ox, one an ass – and made to sit backwards on donkeys; then they had to spend the day being dragged around Lahore, complete with ears and tail and pelted and booed by the populace. The hot sun caused the skins to shrink, and one of them died of suffocation. Khusrau's punishment was to ride along a street – on an elephant – lined with stakes on which his followers had been impaled alive. After that, he was kept in chains for a year.

Incredibly, he had still failed to learn his lesson. In the following year, 1607, he encouraged a plot to assassinate his father. The four ringleaders were put to death, and Jahangir ordered Khusrau to be blinded. This effectively ended Khusrau's hopes of succeeding his father as emperor.

So Shah Jahan was now a clear front runner in the succession stakes. He had always been a bright child, a favourite of his grandfather the great Akbar. Now he consolidated his position by scoring some brilliant military triumphs. First he forced the submission of the ancient kingdom of Rajasthan – a feat which both his father and grandfather had tried and failed. He then staged another remarkable campaign in which he secured the troubled frontiers in the south. He not only persuaded the notoriously rebellious rulers of the Deccan to negotiate terms but also managed to extract from them a vast quantity of jewels and goods as tribute to the Emperor. On his return he was given a kind of Roman triumph and allowed the unprecedented honour of sitting in the Emperor's presence – his chair being placed next to the throne.

Understandably, all this began to worry the Empress. Because of his alcoholism and drug addiction, her husband's health was frail. Which meant that, if he died, she would cease to be empress, and be replaced by her niece Taj. And it would be hard to surrender power. Her husband's court had a splendour that outshone Cleopatra's. When the Emperor was on the move, he was literally accompanied by a small town. The procession of horses, camels, elephants and bullocks was so long that it took twelve hours to pass any given point. When they camped for the night, the 'town' was twenty miles in circumference. In the centre was the Emperor's enclosure, consisting of a sort of portable palace made of wood, several halls, a mosque and – of course – a harem. The bathhouses were drawn on wheels by elephants. A hundred thousand bullocks loaded with grain were necessary to feed this vast horde. Contemplating her husband's power and wealth, the Empress must have felt that it was highly unreasonable to expect her to give it up simply because her husband was dead.

The empress had already hedged her bets by marrying her daughter to Prince Shahriyar. Now she began plotting to try and make sure that Shahriyar should succeed his father on the throne – in which case, the Empress would continue to rule. Shah Jahan felt threatened by all this, but there was little he could do about it. His father adored the Empress, and if he showed open hostility, she might turn his father against him. It was rather like musical chairs; he simply had to hope that, when the music stopped, he would be near enough to the throne to fling himself into it.

This is why when, in 1620, his father ordered him to go back to the Deccan and subdue the rebels all over again, Shah Jahan began to brood on rebellion. In spite of his blindness, the cultured and good-natured Khusrau had many supporters at court, and if Jahangir died, he might well seize the throne. At which point, Shah Jahan had the inspired idea of suggesting that Khusrau should accompany him to the Deccan. He approached Jahangir when he was drunk – which was most of the time – and got permission. In effect, Khusrau was now his hostage.

Subduing the enemy proved unexpectedly easy. Like his father, Shah Jahan travelled with a kind of portable town. (Taj and their two children accompanied them reclining in howdahs on the backs of elephants.) When they arrived in the Deccan, the sight of Shah Jahan's army advancing upon them so alarmed the rebels that they soon agreed to another treaty. His father was delighted, and sent him generous presents from the court (which was then in Agra). But the news that accompanied them was not good; the Emperor was again in poor health. Worse still, some of Shah Jahan's lands were being transferred to his younger brother Shanyar. Shah Jahan's response was to murder his brother Khusrau, to make sure he could never become a contender for the throne. He sent his father a message saying that Khusrau had died of colic. It was the first time – though not the last – that this kind of fratricidal brutality had erupted into the family of the Moghuls.

Soon after this, Jahangir learned that the Persians were marching on Kandahar, a rich trading post on the caravan route. He mobilized an army, and sent a message to Shah Jahan to bring his own troops to join it. For the first time, Shah Jahan chose to defy his father – he refused to go unless he could have sole command of the army. (His reasoning was that, as the commander of a large army, he would be in a powerful bargaining position if his father died.) The Empress was probably delighted by this development – it made it easy to persuade Jahangir that his son should be treated as a rebel and an outcast. Shah Jahan received a stern message forbidding him to enter his father's presence; he tried to apologize but it was too late. Jahangir sent his general Mahabat Khan to bring the rebel to heel.

For three years, Shah Jahan and his army were pursued around the country. In each battle or skirmish he came off worst, but was too nimble to be caught. Finally, when he got tired of running, he sued for peace. The Emperor, equally tired of trying to destroy his favourite son – and aware that his own death could not be long delayed – agreed to surprisingly lenient terms. Shah Jahan was virtually banished by being appointed governor of Balaghat, a remote district. The Empress added the condition that Shah Jahan's two young sons, aged eight and ten, must be sent to court as hostages. The two children were placed in the care of the Empress – an alarming prospect in view of the political situation; but Shah Jahan felt he could trust his family – even the Empress. They did not possess his kind of ruthlessness.

Back in Lahore, strange things were happening. The Empress had finally overreached herself. Concerned that Mahabat Khan – the general who had been chasing Shah Jahan – was becoming too powerful, she began to plot against him, accusing him of dishonesty. At her suggestion, Jahangir appointed him governor to remote Bengal. The general apparently accepted this, and came to Lahore to explain himself – bringing 5,000 men. Jahangir sent him a message to wait until he was summoned. And since the general seemed to be unthreatening, Asaf Khan made the mistake of withdrawing the royal troops across the river.

The general then rode into the almost undefended royal camp, and persuaded Jahangir to return with him to his own camp. In effect, he had kidnapped the Emperor. The Empress and her brother launched an attack, and were beaten; she and Asaf Khan were taken prisoner. But the general assured them he did not regard them as prisoners of war, but as his guests. In retrospect it is hard to see what he had in mind – perhaps he merely wanted to be the power behind the throne. The camp moved north to Kabul, with the imperial army trailing along behind, apparently unaware that anything was wrong. Meanwhile, the Empress plotted and schemed harder than she had ever plotted and schemed in her life. As they were on their way back from Kabul, the Emperor announced that he wished to review the Empress's forces, and asked the general to take his own forces a few miles away, so the two armies could not quarrel. The general complied – and continued to retreat as fast as he could. Realizing that his 'kidnapping' was an act of treason, he made his way to Shah Jahan's headquarters, and offered an alliance. And the Emperor went off north to Kashmir, where it was cool and his asthma improved. There his condition grew worse, and in October 1627 he died.

Now it was the Empress's brother, Asaf Khan, who realized that they were in a dangerous position. If Shahriyar had been there, they could have proclaimed him emperor, and continued to rule as the power behind the throne. But Shahriyar was in the Punjab, whose climate was supposed to be good for the odd form of leprosy he had developed – which made his hair fall out until his head was as bald as an egg. The Empress managed to send him a hasty message to mobilize his forces. Meanwhile, her brother had proclaimed the young son of Khusrau, Dawar Bakhsh, the new emperor, and showed his annoyance at his sister's interference by placing her under house arrest. Then he marched off against the feeble Prince Shahriyar and beat him easily.

Now he had had time to think, Asaf realized he had made a mistake. Shah Jahan and General Mahabat Khan together would undoubtedly be too strong for him. So he sent Shah Jahan a message proclaiming his loyalty.

Now, once more, Shah Jahan revealed that he was capable of ruthless brutality. He sent a message indicating that he wanted Shahriyar and Dawar Bakhsh murdered, as well as two other possible contenders for the throne – sons of his deceased uncle Daniyal. Asaf carried out these orders; and in return, was made chief minister of the new emperor, Shah Jahan. The general was also rewarded with a desirable governorship. And so, at last, Shah Jahan was the Great Moghul.

He might have felt justified in executing the Empress who had made his life so miserable. But after killing five of his relatives, he seems to have experienced a return of the traditional Moghul clemency – after all, he was not a barbarian like his ancestors Genghis Khan and Tamurlane – and awarded her a generous pension instead. She was allowed to spend the remainder of her life building a magnificent tomb for her husband at Lahore.

Meanwhile, there had been an emotional reunion with the two young princes – Dara and Aurengzeb – who had been held hostage. After years of wandering around as a homeless nomad, Shah Jahan was at last secure. He was still only thirty-six, and in excellent health. Now at last he should have been able to settle down with his wife and family at Agra, and enjoy the fruits of his long struggle. But it was not to be. After a mere eighteen months as emperor – aided in all his decisions by his adored wife – he was forced to march off to the Deccan to put down rebellion. And since he hated to be parted from his wife and children, he took them with him. It was a mistake he would regret for the rest of his days. During the expedition, Taj became pregnant with their fourteenth child. Swaying around on the back of an elephant – even in a howdah – was hardly the ideal way to relax during pregnancy. In June 1631, Taj died during childbirth.

Her husband was devastated; he had gained the world and lost what he loved most. He was so heartbroken that he ceased to eat. For the next two years he wandered around like a shadow, wearing the simplest clothes and avoiding rich food. Soldiering – which had cost him his wife – ceased to interest him. In future, he left it to his son Aurengzeb, who was fifteen at the time of his mother's death. (The Moghul princes began fighting early – sixteen was the usual age – although their generals really did most of the work.) Finally, he recovered from his grief enough to continue building the magnificent pleasure garden which he had intended for his wife; it would now become her tomb.

During the next twelve years vast sums of money were spent bringing together the best artists and craftsmen. Master builders, masons, inlayers and caligraphers as well as the materials they worked with, came from all over India and Central Asia. In 1632, the year work began, the English traveller Peter Mundy described how the building was being created 'with extraordinary diligence, with gold and silver esteemed common metal and marble but as ordinary stone'. The Taj Mahal employed 20,000 workmen and cost the equivalent of £16,000,000. The magnificent grounds and gardens that surround it took a further ten years to complete. By 1643 the building was sufficiently complete for the annual memorial service for Taj to be held there for the first time.

Standing on a marble terrace overlooking the Yamuna river outside Agra, the superb mausoleum is regarded as the greatest of Moghul buildings. Its beauty results not only from the fine balance of its parts, which take on a new and enchanting appearance from every angle or approach, but

The Taj Mahal at Agra in India

also from the opalescent marble surface, which continually reflects subtle changes of light.

Regrettably, the death of Taj was only the first of the tribulations of Shah Jahan's reign. The remainder were largely his own fault, as he proceeded to repeat his father's mistakes. His eldest son Dara was his favourite – but then, *he* had also been his own father's favourite, and he had rebelled. To prevent Dara from rebelling, he kept him close under his eye at court, and spoiled him with presents and honours. His younger son Aurengzeb, he sent off to fight his battles, forgetting that a prince who becomes a successful military leader is in a better position to challenge his father than one who is kept at home.

Aurengzeb was a rather dour character, a fanatical Moslem, unlike his easygoing elder brother, who had the same broad religious tolerance of the great Akbar. (Aurengzeb called him an atheist.) Shah Jahan was not particularly fond of him, and allowed this to show. In 1644, when Dara and Aurengzeb were having a bitter disagreement, Shah Jahan dismissed Aurengzeb and deprived him of his rank and allowances. He reinstated him a few months later, but Aurengzeb saw it as an omen for the future, and took note.

Shah Jahan sent Aurengzeb to try and take Kandahar; when he failed, he was recalled in disgrace – to his brother's malicious amusement. Dara boasted he could take it in a week, and set off with an even bigger and better army; but to Aurengzeb's delight, he was equally unsuccessful. Dara now began to take a spiteful pleasure in frustrating and tormenting his brother. On two occasions, Aurengzeb was about to win campaigns in the Deccan when his father halted them – after intervention by Dara, who persuaded him to accept money instead of victory.

Then, in 1657, Shah Jahan fell ill. Always something of a sexual athlete, he apparently took a strong aphrodisiac to enhance his performance in the harem, and it caused him to retain urine for three days until he was in agony. Rumours of his death flew around Delhi. In fact, he had appointed Dara his deputy during his illness, and when he recovered, retired to Agra, probably glad to leave his favourite son in charge. Dara's three younger brothers – there were two more princes in addition to Aurengzeb – decided to march on Delhi. One of them – Shah Shuja – was defeated by Dara's son. But the other two, Aurengzeb and Murad, joined forces, and defeated Dara's army. Dara had to flee. Aurengzeb besieged his father in his fort at Agra, and forced him to surrender by cutting off his water supply. Shah Jahan became the prisoner of the son he liked least. Then Aurengzeb went on to draw the teeth of his rival Murad by inviting him to supper, getting him drunk (as a strict Moslem Aurengzeb was teetotal) and taking him prisoner. After that, Aurengzeb proclaimed himself emperor.

Dara was also captured and beheaded – when the head was sent to Aurengzeb, he refused to look at it on the grounds that Dara had been an infidel. Murad was also executed on a legal pretext. And so Aurengzeb continued the tradition of murder started by his father. He also imprisoned his son for the rest of his life.

Shah Jahan was at least spared. He was allowed to live out the remaining eight years of his life in peace in his fort in Agra, within sight of his wife's tomb. One chronicler says that he spent his remaining years in debauchery in his harem, but this seems doubtful – at sixty-six, his bladder problems refused to go away, and his sexual powers were on the wane. Nursed by his eldest daughter, who had taken the place of Taj as first lady, he became unexpectedly pious, and spent his days studying the Koran – and no doubt reflecting on his stupidity at having made the same mistakes as his father. He died peacefully in 1666, at the age of seventy-three.

Aurengzeb's life was as troubled as that of his father. Having murdered his way to the throne, he spent his life fighting battles largely provoked by his own aggressiveness and religious intolerance. He soldiered on – literally – into his eighties, and when he died at the age of eighty-eight, the age of the Great Moghuls was virtually over.

Chapter Six

The Amazing Jane Digby

Jane Digby was a great romantic and also a great adventurer. Romance and adventure are the twin themes that run through the story of her life, as she sought – and eventually found – true love. For a woman whose behaviour would scandalize her Victorian contemporaries, Jane Digby's background was impeccable. Born in 1807, she was the daughter of Lady Andover and Admiral Digby. Most of her childhood was spent in Holkham Hall, the imposing Norfolk home of her maternal grandfather the Earl of Leicester. She had a happy and normal childhood, playing games, riding ponies and wandering freely in the countryside with her two brothers. One of them later recalled that she was far more adventurous than they were: she could climb higher, ride faster and shoot a pheasant at a brisker gallop. When she was ten, her parents decided that this tomboy life was unsuitable for a young lady of the upper class, and a governess – Miss Steele – appeared at Holkham. She was pleased to find Jane 'an intelligent child with a natural aptitude for languages and a love of literature well beyond her years'. Jane had a natural confidence that sprang from the fact that she had been surrounded by admiration from birth. She was a born beauty, with large blue eyes, fine, even features, translucent complexion and masses of soft blonde hair; she was also tall and graceful, with a suppleness and physical energy which hardly diminished throughout her long life.

At sixteen, dressed in white satin and ostrich feathers, she was presented at court, and attracted much favourable comment from the monocled members of England's governing classes. But Miss Steele commented gloomily on the laxness of their morals, and admitted her anxiety about the young girl whose 'imagination and a certain instability of temperament' made her frighteningly vulnerable.

Within a short time Jane was engaged to be married. Edward Laws, Lord Ellenborough was rich, handsome and a thirty-four-year-old widower when he proposed, and Jane's mother had urged her to accept. A contemporary diarist, Edmond About, described Jane at that period, '. . . all pink and white, like a book bound in muslin, full of white pages . . . . Lord Ellenborough must have been very much attracted to her to contemplate such an uneven marriage.' But his interests soon dwindled. He was a cold, unemotional man, whose interests were centred entirely on his political career. Yet even as a politician he was thoroughly unpopular, disliked in the house for his acid tongue and lack of humour, and also for his arrogance, shabby behaviour and inordinate vanity about his wavy brown hair.

From the beginning the marriage was a failure: Ellenborough was both pompous and dull – a disastrous mixture for a girl of Jane's lively and ardent temperament. Gossips declared that he was impotent; certainly before the honeymoon was over Jane found herself left alone most of the time at their homes at Roehampton or London. In 1828 Jane disproved the malicious rumours by bearing him a son, Arthur, and Lord Ellenborough noted complacently in his diary that he would make the boy into a politician.

With an heir provided he thereafter paid even less attention to his wife, and ignored the protestations of her parents that she needed more attention if she was not to fall into unsuitable company. Jane herself soon learned to accept the situation, and was soon surrounded by the kind of admirers her parents feared. The young men of Regency London had two main diversions: gambling and love affairs

74

(with the occasional duel to add a touch of danger), and Miss Steele's fears soon proved to be well-founded. There was a certain amount of censorious gossip, but the general opinion was that if Lord Ellenborough chose to neglect such a pretty wife, he had only himself to blame. Jane soon became a regular visitor at two of the most influential salons, and it was at one of these that she met Prince Felix Swartzenberg, recently appointed to London as Secretary of the Austrian Embassy.

Neither of them seems to have taken the least trouble to conceal their affair. Although adultery was commonplace at the time, discretion was expected, and their openness caused offence. There was gossip about meetings in his Harley Street rooms, and about how, through a half-drawn blind, he had been seen lacing her stays. Then there was the visit to the Brighton hotel where the Prince had visited the lady for tea and not emerged until breakfast. Some added that she had climbed on to a rooftop and shouted that she loved him. Lord Ellenborough remained resolutely deaf and did nothing – a factor which was to tell against him in the divorce proceedings which followed.

Jane's family were horrified, and having failed to pursuade her husband to act, they swooped upon their now obviously pregnant daughter and spirited her off to a cottage in Ilfracombe, where she was guarded and lectured by the aptly named 'Steely'.

In the meantime, the Prince had found the emotional pace of the affair exhausting, and had fled to Paris to recover. He had reckoned without Jane's 'imagination and instability of temperament' – and also the fact that she loved him. When she arrived in Paris she was distressed to find that her lover's ardour had noticeably cooled. Looking at him through less adoring eyes, she concluded that he was neither idealistic nor truly passionate, besides which, he was a Catholic, whose faith would prevent him from

marrying a divorcee. Swartzenberg was willing to acknow-
ledge that she was among the greatest beauties of her
period, and she had given up everything for him – fortune,
good name, friends and family; all the same, he felt that she
was lacking in that most essential of female qualities, tact.
But he recognized that his duties as a gentleman demanded
that he should install her in his apartment. In the Paris
salons they frequented, it was observed that the Prince was
seldom to be found at home, and that even at the time of his
mistress's confinement, he was 'going about flirting'. The
birth of a daughter did little to bring them closer, and the
liaison that had begun so romantically drooped into sad
decline. In due course he walked out again, this time for
good.

The Paris of the 1830s glittered with brilliant personalities
like Berlioz, Chopin, Delacroix, Balzac, and with the salons
that centred around them. It was a carnival city given over
to masked balls and riverside picnics. All this provided Jane
with some consolation for the Prince's indifference. Paris
differed from London in that here there was a broad
overlap between respectable society and the 'vie de
bohème'. As Prince Swartzenberg's mistress there were a
number of houses from which the ex-Lady Ellenborough
was debarred, but among artists and writers, musicians and
philosophers, she found friends who regarded her notoriety
as an asset. This new generation, who liked to refer to
themselves as Romantics, were more stimulating than
anything to be found in London, and in this atmosphere,
Jane developed into an outstanding conversationalist. Her
admirers agreed that she was witty, well-read and charmingly good-natured. But after Swartzenberg's departure,
Jane herself began to tire of being liked and admired, and
decided it was time to move on. Abandoning her maternal
duties to the Prince's obliging family, she set off to see the
rest of the world.

Jane's friend and lover King Ludwig I of Bavaria lavished huge sums of money on rebuilding Munich in the Greek style, rushing between Athens and Rome, importing statues and chunks of ancient buildings. But he insisted that his home be run on rigid economy. The royal children ate black bread and when the King requested onions with his dinner the royal cooks protested that they could not possibly serve such things on their budget.

Her arrival in Munich, the capital of Bavaria, caused an instant stir. She was invited to court, and at once became the mistress of the amiable and eccentric King Ludwig I. He added her portrait to his gallery of beautiful women – the contemplation of which, he explained, brought him inspiration – and he encouraged her to take lessons in sculpture, painting and classical Greek. Ludwig was passionate about ancient Greek culture, and lavished incredible sums rebuilding Munich in neoclassical style. But while Jane was fond of the King, she had better sense than to fall in love with him. Being a royal mistress seemed to her a fairly trivial occupation. She explained in her diary: '. . . my nature is to consider love as all in all without this feeling life is a dreary void . . . loving and being loved is to me as the air I breathe . . .'

While out riding, she met the Baron Carl-Theodore von Venningen, a Bavarian nobleman. He was young and handsome, rich and of suitably ancient lineage. Within a short time he had proposed to her. Jane was hesitant. Perhaps still thinking of Swartzenberg, she wrote: 'there exists something in a first passion that no time can efface.' Her parents sent frantic messages urging her to accept. She wrote to the King – with whom she was always to remain on the friendliest of terms: '[perhaps] love as I picture it is not necessary in marriage; the Baron's whole conduct is faultless, but in love I am not.' Presently, however, Jane's English relatives learned with relief that she was married. In Munich some thought that the marriage had been arranged by the King so that his child should be born in wedlock, but the birth of the child proved them wrong, for he was the image of the Baron.

The couple moved to Sicily, and for two years lived contentedly in the sunshine. When another child was born they decided to return to the family estates and Munich. But Jane was again becoming restless; the regular pattern of married life failed to satisfy an obscure craving for adventure, changing scenes, even danger. In her diary she wrote of her husband: 'His noble qualities are justly esteemed by me and I am attached to him from affection and habit, but his lack of demonstration of warmth stifles the passion I could feel and once felt and returned would prevent me wandering even in thought.'

Now at this time King Ludwig's son Otho had been crowned king of Greece, so there was a regular exchange of visitors between Munich and Athens. One of the most attractive of the young Greeks to arrive in Munich was Count Spyridon Theotoki. A romantic figure, born into a poor but noble family in Corfu, he seemed to embody all the colour and adventure that her life as a Munich matron denied her. They met at a court ball, and were instantly attracted to one another.

Shortly after this, the von Venningens left for their country estate in Baden. Theotoki followed, staying nearby in Heidelberg. There were secret assignations, romantic rides through the forests, from which Jane sometimes returned at dawn. The Baron, suspecting nothing, continued with Germanic thoroughness to make the rounds of his estates. The Greek count begged her to come away with him, and Jane found it increasingly difficult to dissemble. Inevitably, the Baron became suspicious. When, during a court ball for the King of Prussia, the couple slipped away, the Baron noticed their absence and he set off in pursuit in a racing carriage that soon overtook them. The avenging husband challenged Theotoki to a duel. At the first shot Theotoki fell, wounded in the chest and apparently dying. As he lay bleeding in Jane's arms he managed to swear to the Baron that their love had been innocent, that nothing dishonourable had taken place. Unable to believe that a dying man would risk his immortal soul by lying, the Baron was seized with contrition. He ordered Theotoki to be conveyed to his house, where night and day the distraught Jane nursed him. There were a series of harrowing, remorseful farewells between the Baron and the Count, but fate withheld the emotional climax, and – NOT entirely to the Baron's delight – the Count began to recover.

It was a difficult situation – a woman required to choose between two men who each wished to behave more honourably and nobly than the other. The passionate Theotoki and the increasingly impatient von Venningen awaited her decision. Predictably, Jane finally decided in favour of poverty and romance. The Baron, realizing that his wife was in love with Theotoki, tried hard to warn her, but finally resigned himself to separation. He wrote: 'I hope you find . . . the happiness I tried in vain to give you. I have ever loved with heart and soul and all my faculties only you alone. No woman will ever possess me as you have possessed me. I have friends, a few, perhaps I will have a mistress, but I will never again have another Jane.'

She and Theotoki went to Paris, where they lived happily for several years. But she was saddened at the pain she had caused the Baron, and to the end of her life remained in affectionate correspondence with him. Eventually the delicate matter of Jane's divorce was settled and the couple were able to marry in the Greek Orthodox Church. They then left Paris and went to live in Corfu, where the Count's family welcomed Jane. Here, amid the beautiful land and seascapes, cypress trees and sunshine, she felt happier and more fulfilled than ever before. A son was born, and named Leonidas, and Jane, to her own surprise, found herself a devoted mother. She wrote to her brother: 'You will never believe how domestic I am and what a good mother I am being. I feel very much at home in this rugged country. I would be content to stay here for the rest of my life.' Back at home, the rest of family heaved a sigh of relief.

But it was not to be. When Count Theotoki was appointed aide de camp to King Otho, they surrendered the peace and simplicity of Corfu and moved to Athens. Here in the capital city life was once again full of distractions, and since Jane was the most attractive woman at court, she was soon surrounded by admirers; so, in fact, was the handsome Theotoki. It was soon clear that King Otho was as enchanted with her as his father had been. Queen Amalie was furious, and her bitterness was increased by the fact that the Countess Theotoki had not only stolen the affections of her husband, but of her people as well. When the Countess rode out, cheering crowds would refer to her as 'the Queen of Love and Beauty'. Jane seemed to have the power of causing trouble wherever she went.

At home the Theotokis' lives became more and more separate. Then, while in Italy taking the waters at Lucca, the first and only real tragedy of Jane's life occurred. Six-year-old Leonidas, sleeping on the top floor of their rented house, heard his mother welcoming guests downstairs and tried to slide down the banisters to join her. He overbalanced and fell to his death on the marble floor at her feet. She never recovered from this loss. With their child's death the marriage fell apart. For a long while Jane stayed indoors.

The Amazing Jane Digby

When at last she returned to Athens, she was alone for she and Theotoki had separated. Jane lived quietly with her faithful French maid Eugenie, who had been with her since Paris.

Nineteenth-century Athens was a new city. Otho had chosen the site of the capital partly in deference to his father's antiquarian interests (though very few Athenians were in the least interested in 'the ruins'); until recently it had been a quiet fishing village. Now it was rapidly developing into a cosmopolitan city with new buildings in the classical style, and an intermixture of races that converged in a culture that was a mixture of East and West. The city was surrounded by rugged hills and mountains, but the citizens hardly ever ventured into the surrounding country; almost everything they needed arrived by sea at the busy waterfront.

The most obviously striking of the races in the city was the Pelikares, Albanian mercenaries who had fought bravely and effectively in the war for independence. These warriors were volatile and unpredictable, and it was to ensure their good behaviour that King Otho appointed the chief of the Pelikares, General Xristodolous Hadji Petros, as aide de camp to replace Theotoki. Hadji Petros was an impressive figure; moustachioed, bristling with pistols and knives, he towered over the tallest men at court. He wore Albanian costume – all red and gold embroideries – and behaved in as princely a fashion as he dressed. At sixty plus, he was still handsome, ferocious and attractive to women. The Pelikares were legendary for their ruthlessness and daring, and when they swept down from the mountains, reeking of garlic and wearing great fur cloaks which made them look like bears, there was much heart-fluttering excitement among the ladies of the court. It was even rumoured that the Queen had a tender spot for Hadji Petros . . .

True Love Stories

Jane made the acquaintance of the Pelikares chieftain through his son. The young boy was the age Leonidas would have been if he had lived, and Jane became fond of him. Within a short time Hadji Petros had asked her to come and live with him and his men in the mountains; and since she never turned down an opportunity for new experience, she accepted. Always strong and athletic, Jane, now aged forty-five, galloped through the rough country, sharing the adventures of the wild horsemen, living on roast lamb and retsina, and sleeping in camp surrounded by brigands. She revelled in the freedom, and felt more alive as the mistress of a chieftain than she ever had as a wife.

It was when Jane began to arrange a divorce from Theotoki so that she could marry her brigand that the Queen struck. She persuaded her husband to dismiss Hadji Petros as his aide de camp. The wily chieftain responded with a sycophantic letter to the Queen: 'If I am this woman's lover, it is not for love's sake, but purely for self-interest. She is wealthy, I am poor . . . I have a position to maintain and children to educate.' The Queen lost no time in publishing the letter. But Jane was not worried by this; her nature was generous and trusting, and perhaps it was the unscrupulous bandit aspect of Hadji Petros that she most admired. Ignoring the outrage at court, she rented adjoining houses in a quiet part of Athens – she and Eugenie in one, Hadji Petros and his men next door. Financial questions never bothered her greatly, and she was fortunate that so much of her life was spent in countries where her allowance of £3,000 a year made her seem wealthy.

Her maid Eugenie must have found it difficult living with twenty or so rough, hard-drinking, violent men. They camped in the gardens, built fires on the lawns and roared and shouted late into the night. For her the last straw was Hadji Petros. Eugenie told Jane she could stand it no more – he was continually trying to molest her, and she had to fight him off with her fists. Jane was her usual decisive self. She and Eugenie packed and disappeared overnight without explanation. The public humiliation of the letter meant nothing; but this private humiliation was intolerable.

They sailed for Syria. There was no going back to England – Jane's family had given her up, and turned her picture to the wall; only her loving brother kept in touch. In any case, she wanted to get away from echoes of the past. Heartbroken, she felt that at forty-six, her life was over; all she could see before her was a solitary old age. But since her interest in travel and archaeology was undiminished, she decided to visit the classical ruins at Palmyra in northern Syria. The British consul at Damascus was not at all happy that Countess Theotoki – or Madame Digby, as she now wished to be called – was contemplating the dangerous trip across the desert. The route was controlled by hostile Bedouin tribes, and even with a 'safe passage' and a guide, it was still dangerous. Such things never deterred Jane, and finally the consul was persuaded to recommend a Bedouin guide. He was Sheikh Abdul Medjuel El Mezrab; his tribe controlled the desert around Palmyra and were regarded as honourable, trustworthy and cultivated. The tribe was not rich, but they were an ancient and aristocratic people. Jane wrote in her diary: 'My heart warms to these wild Arabs. They have many qualities we want in civilized life. Unbounded hospitality, respect for strangers, good faith and simplicity amongst themselves; and a certain high-bred politeness.'

The consul was not surprised to hear that the expedition had run into trouble after only a few days. Jane described what happened in a letter to her brother: 'Suddenly through the evening light, there galloped towards us a party of evil-looking men, yelling and waving their spears in the air. Most of my escort seemed to melt away into the desert. Only Medjuel was left and he defended me fiercely with a passion which appeared to startle the raiding party who finally turned and galloped off.'

It is just possible that the raiders were part of Medjuel's own tribe, and had expected only a token resistance. The English lady would have been robbed and they would share her valuables. But Medjuel put up a genuine defence – behaviour that must have struck the attackers as bewildering loyalty to his client. So they withdrew, and Jane, who revelled in drama, was thrilled.

It seems likely that Medjuel was fascinated by Jane from the first. Now she allowed him to teach her the ways of the desert. They galloped off to visit the ruins and oases, to hunt antelope and wolves, and shoot partridge. Jane described him in her diary: 'Like all Bedouin he is a small man. Very graceful, with a light easy step. His face is really beautiful, perfect oval, long aquiline nose, delicately formed mouth and large black eyes that can be as sweet as a woman's or flash with a fierce wild glance.' Although she noted these things with the practised eye of a connoisseur of men, it seems she was not yet ready to embark upon another relationship, and Medjuel – sensing that if he wanted this extraordinary woman for his own he would need to marry her – took his time. It was almost unthinkable for a Moslem sheikh to marry a Christian, and it is a mark of Jane's exceptional qualities that he should even have contemplated it.

Jane now returned to Damascus, and planned to settle in a house in the Arab quarter, accompanied by Eugenie; but first she had to return to Greece. She stayed in Athens just long enough to settle the matter of her divorce from Count Theotoki, and to cold-shoulder the renewed advances of Hadji Petros. Then, with a sense of relief at having turned her back on her European life for ever, she prepared to fling herself into exploration of her new world of the East.

At this time Syria was virtually unknown to European

travellers, and Jane was only the second woman to travel there alone. (The first was Lady Hester Stanhope.) She plunged into learning Arabic, and prepared to explore the wilderness – to the continued dismay of the British consul. On her second expedition she employed a different guide. She felt as if this harsh, inhospitable country was the home she had been seeking all her life. Certainly, the Europeans who met her found her a striking figure. She exuded health and vitality. Edward Lear records coming across her somewhere near Petra wearing 'a crimson velvet pelisse and green satin riding habit'. She recorded in her diary: '[I have] been travelling along the caravan route between Aleppo and Baghdad. Found a Greek inscription on a rock. Saw tombs hanging from the cliffs at Petra. Did many drawings and watercolours and yesterday on the banks of the Tigris I picked up a porcupine quill. What a journey this would be with someone I really loved, who could understand and return my attachment . . .'

On her way back to Damascus, still far out in the desert, 'a most unexpected event . . . Medjuel came out to meet me, bringing as a present a beautiful Arab mare. He did not say much, but his eyes spoke immense pleasure.' Together they returned to the city, and during the days that followed, Jane discovered that Medjuel had all the qualities she had sought in other men. He had character, integrity, brains and breeding. When he proposed, she accepted unreservedly. She wrote: 'He is a rare and wonderful man . . . I am forty-seven and suddenly I am as much in love as a young girl. If I had neither mirror nor memory I would believe myself to be fifteen years old.'

The British consul was at first speechless, inclined to question her sanity, and wrote a desperate letter to her family in England, begging them to save her from a disastrous fate. Medjuel's own family were also opposed to the marriage – they disapproved of mixed marriages, and regarded Madame Digby as Medjuel's social inferior. But all barriers were swept aside – the consul declining to take further responsibility – and they were married by a Turkish official at a Moslem ceremony. 'Medjuel and I have agreed always to follow our separate religions: neither trying to convert the other.' Certainly, converting Medjuel to Christianity was the last thing on her mind – unlike her friend Isabel Burton, her attitude towards religion was refreshingly practical.

She wrote a glowing letter to her brother, explaining that she and Medjuel would spend half the year living in the desert in black Bedouin tents, and the other half in her house in Damascus. She was determined to live as a true Bedouin wife. Always ready to adapt to new circumstances, she lined her eyes with kohl, got used to wearing the traditional long blue robe of the Bedouin women, had learned to milk the camels. But even as a faithful Bedouin wife, she remained the independent and capable woman she had always been. Her superb horsemanship and her knowledge of doctoring horses (legacies from the stables at Holkham) were greatly valued by the Arabs. She learned to hunt with a falcon or Persian hounds, and to ride on dromedaries as well as on horseback – she was often seen racing ahead of the Bedouins. In Medjuel's tribe she was known as Umn-el-Laban – Mother of Milk, in reference to her white skin.

Her life became increasingly concerned with tribal affairs. There were constant feuds and raids, and hostile tribes would swoop in the night and snatch their best animals. Then Medjuel would ride off to battle with his men, often accompanied by Jane, who proved to be a fearless and capable fighter. Until she was nearly seventy she continued to take part in inter-tribal wars, galloping by Medjuel's side, yelling and waving a spear in true Bedouin fashion.

The Amazing Jane Digby

> True love is like a ghost: everybody talks about it but few have seen it.
>
> *La Rochefoucauld*

No one could claim that Medjuel had married her for her money; in financial matters he remained fiercely independent – the only occasion he accepted help was when she used her money to buy more up-to-date weapons for the tribe.

In 1872, following a particularly serious desert battle, news of Jane's death reached Damascus. Since she was now as well known in the Levant as she had been in Europe, the international press publicized the story. But the report was false, and when at last she rode back into Damascus in triumph with Medjuel she had the doubtful pleasure of reading her own obituary notices. It was racy reading – one writer credited her with six husbands in Italy alone. In England her family winced and shook their heads – even from the grave, it seemed, she created scandal.

At last, after an absence of thirty years, Jane returned to England to sort out her legal affairs and make her will. And although her family – apart from her brother – were still far from happy about the marriage, and preferred to behave as if it had never happened, she was at last reconciled with them.

Medjuel and Jane Digby el Mezrab remained happily married for more than thirty years; it remained a vital and passionate relationship to the end. Looking back on her past life she wrote: 'Had I in early life married the sheikh or a man with a character resembling his, so upright, so truthful, so true, I could not have caused so much grief. Such a companion might have saved me much.'

On 11 August 1881 after a short attack of dysentery, Jane

True Love Stories

Digby died at her house in Damascus, with Medjuel beside her. Even as she made her last appearance on earth there was drama. During the funeral procession, Medjuel leapt from the carriage with an electrifying shriek and ran off like a madman. Then, as the service in the Christian cemetery was almost over, the shaken mourners heard the sound of galloping hooves, and Medjuel, astride Jane's favourite mare, rode up to the open grave. He paused for a while, gazing at the coffin, then turned and galloped away.

Chapter Seven

Richard and Isabel Burton

When Isabel Arundell was in her mid teens, her family rented a country house in Essex – they wanted to save money before launching their daughter in London society the following year. Feeling that this would mark the end of her freedom, Isabel spent her days dreaming in her bedroom, wandering around the countryside and reading in the library. It was there that she discovered Disraeli's novel *Tancred*, a tale of a young aristocrat who finds spirtual fulfilment in the Arabian desert, and it fascinated her so much that she read it over and over again. Her daydreams were full of Bedouin encampments and starry desert nights, and tall dignified Arabs with dark eyes.

So when, in the local woods, she discovered a gypsy encampment, she found it irresistible. She began to spend her days there, drawn towards this dark, exotic people by some deep romantic attraction. Her parents would have been horrified, but Isabel didn't care. She was going through the 'awkward age', overweight, self-critical and obstinate, and the gypsies somehow symbolized the life she wanted to lead.

On the day she had to leave for London, a gypsy fortune teller named Hagar Burton cast her horoscope. It was everything that Isabel wanted to hear.

'You will cross the sea, and be in the same town with your Destiny and know it not. Every obstacle will rise up against you, and such a combination of circumstances that it will require all your courage, energy and intelligence to meet them. You will fix your eye on your polar star, and you will go for that without looking right or left. You will bear the name of our tribe, and be right proud of it. Your life is all wandering, change and adventure. One soul in two bodies, in life or death; never long apart. Show this to the man you take for your husband.'

It was a strange prophecy for a girl who belonged to a respectable middle-to-upper-class family, relatives of the Earl of Arundell. The Arundells appear in English history as courtiers and statesmen from the time of William the Conqueror. They had always been devout Catholics, and Isabel was no exception. Born in London in 1831, she had spent her childhood in the comfortable – but not luxurious – surroundings of Cumberland Place; her father was one of the poorer members of the family and ran a wine business.

Like any child of a moderately well-off Victorian family, Isabel grew up with nannies and walks in the park and holidays in the country, when she rode a fat pony to hounds and called on the poor with baskets of food.

Now she had turned dreamy and difficult, her mother was concerned. It was so important to make a good impression in one's first season. But she need not have worried. Isabel's debut was brilliant. With her blonde hair and junoesque figure, she was greatly in demand among the eligible young bachelors looking for a well-connected wife. Her connection with the Earl of Arundell went a long way towards mitigating her lack of dowry. So Isabel received much gratifying notice – which she treated with an indifference that baffled her mother and aunts.

They pleaded with her in vain. Isabel had a clear idea of her ideal man, and was certain that he would not be found at fashionable parties or the opera. She described him in her diary: 'six feet in height, he has not an ounce of fat on him; he has broad and muscular shoulders, a powerful, deep

Richard and Isabel Burton

chest; he is a Hercules of manly strength. He has black hair, a brown complexion, a clever forehead, sagacious eyebrows, large, black, wondrous eyes – those strange eyes you dare not take yours from off them – with long lashes. He is a soldier and a man; he is accustomed to command and to be obeyed. His religion is like my own, free, liberal and generous minded . . . he is one of those strong men who lead, the master mind who governs . . .' How many other girls have dreamed about such romantic supermen, then gone on to marry someone in the City or Civil Service? Not Isabel. Some curious instinct had led her to pen an accurate description of her future husband.

When the season ended without a match, her disappointed family made the best of it, and moved to the English colony in Boulogne for two years, where eligible bachelors were also to be found, and living was cheaper than in London. Here life was quiet, with afternoons of embroidery, pleasant, gossipy teas with the families of retired officers, and healthy walks in the sea air all horribly dull for someone dreaming of dark-complexioned heroes and Arabian adventure.

It was while walking along the ramparts one afternoon with her sister that Isabel came face to face with her destiny. Richard Burton had been recently sent back from army service in India, in somewhat dubious circumstances. He was twenty-eight years old and a bachelor. He was also tall, dark-skinned, and had the brooding eyes of Isabel's dream hero. The pretty, buxom, pink-skinned girl caught his attention as she passed and Burton, who had been practising hypnotism, threw her one of his magnetic glances. Isabel seems to have had no doubt whatever that this was the man foretold by Hagar Burton. When they were a little distance away Isabel turned to her sister and said, 'That man will marry me.'

The next day they met again at the same place. This time

he wrote a note on the wall: 'May I speak with you?' She picked up the chalk and wrote, 'No, mother will be angry.' Her mother following behind, found the messages and, as predicted, was furious.

It was a week later before Isabel heard his name, and it merely confirmed what she knew by instinct: that this was the man Hagar Burton had foretold. The occasion was a tea dance given by her cousin Louisa. 'There', wrote Isabel, 'was Richard like a star among rushlights! . . . he waltzed with me once, and spoke to me several times, and I kept my sash where he put his arm round my waist . . . and my gloves which his hands had clasped. I never wore them again.'

She subsequently made frequent trips to the ramparts hoping to catch another glimpse of him and thrill to the sound of his rich and exceptionally pleasant voice. It happened several times, and she recorded that she would 'turn hot and cold, dizzy and faint, sick and trembling'. Her mother observed these symptoms, and promptly called a doctor, who diagnosed indigestion and prescribed pills (which Isabel sensibly threw on the fire).

The object of her adoration seems to have failed to notice her, and later he could not even recall having met her. Burton had many things to occupy his time – writing, fencing, riding, studying foreign languages, and planning an expedition to the Moslem holy city of Mecca, where non-Moslems were strictly forbidden and likely to be put to death. Isabel saw far too little of him before the family returned to London.

For four more years Isabel waited patiently, totally convinced that Burton was her destiny, and that one day he would return. This may seem odd, in view of the fact that she had received not the slightest encouragement, but she was immensely strong willed, and her devout Catholicism seems to have endowed her with the power of faith. Even

> Love is a sport in which the hunter must contrive
> to have the quarry in pursuit.
>
> *Kerr*

so, there must have been moments when she wondered if this was all self-delusion, as we can see from this diary entry: 'If Richard and I never marry, God will cause us to meet in the next world, we cannot be parted; we belong to each other.'

Isabel, now over twenty-one, continued to receive attentions from various suitable admirers, but – to the despair and incomprehension of her parents, who had no idea that she considered herself betrothed – continued to reject them all. Instead she lived a sedate and ladylike existence at home, rereading *Tancred* and devouring everything Burton had written (*Falconry in the Valley of the Indus, A Complete System of Bayonet Exercise*, his anthropological study *The Jats of Scinde*, and much more) and caused raised eyebrows at afternoon teas with her glowing testimonials to these works. She followed with pride every fragment of news about him and became something of an expert on his life.

What information there was would hardly have reassured her family. Born in Torquay, in Devon, in 1821, Burton was of a mixed English, Irish and French ancestry. His father's army career was unspectacular and ended in early retirement; the family lived abroad – in France and Italy – because it was cheaper. He and his brother had little regular education – wearing out a series of tutors – but acquired an early mastery of fencing and shooting; they rode, smoked, gambled and experimented in all the available vices, until their father sent them off to Oxford and Cambridge respectively; in the hope that separating them would have a sobering influence.

True Love Stories

Burton loathed Oxford, finding his fellow students dull ('I have fallen among grocers') and his tutors intolerant of his exuberant and overconfident behaviour and curious pronunciation of Latin and Greek. But he displayed remarkable linguistic ability and taught himself Arabic and Hindustani. Finally after many clashes with authority, he was sent down for attending a horse race when he should have been at a lecture. His father had hoped he would make a career of the Church, but that option was closed by his expulsion from Oxford, and Burton was able to choose his own career – that of an officer in the Bombay Native Infantry.

Greedy for knowledge and experience, he found that India opened up the possibility of the kind of life he had always wanted to live. Everything about the landscape and the people entranced him as they would later entrance Rudyard Kipling. His major disappointment was to learn that all the battles were over; the Afghan war had just ended. But he devoted his immense nervous energy to learning Persian, Punjabi and eight or nine Indian dialects. He studied with Hindu gurus; from his Sepoy troops he learned wrestling, the sword dance, lance thrusts, and fighting from horseback; from his Indian mistresses he learned the amazing subtleties of Eastern lovemaking; and in the markets and villages he learned to handle snakes, perform fakir magic, and the art of poetic narration. While on sick leave in Goa – supposedly recuperating – he formulated a romantic plan to rescue an attractive young woman from confinement in a nunnery, but in the dark, entered the wrong room and carried off the irate sub-prioress.

His superiors admired his initiative but deplored his eccentric behaviour. He was an indispensible interpreter and a useful spy, but his endless curiosity and passion for information made him a source of potential embarrass-

ment. Appointed official interpreter to the major-general,
he was often entrusted with confidential missions, and
acquired such mastery of the art of disguise that he
frequently passed his commanding officer without being
recognized. He found the markets and back streets a source
of important information, and warned of the Indian Mutiny
long before it broke out – in fact, if his information had not
been ignored, it could have prevented the mutiny.

It was one of these 'confidential' missions which led to
the termination of his military career. The authorities were
concerned that British rule was being undermined by
rampant moral corruption due to the sheer number of
homosexual brothels in Bombay. Burton was sent to
investigate, a task he performed with such efficiency that
the brothels were closed down; his hair-raising report,
glorying in the kind of frankness that made Victorians
blush, was subsequently filed in the back of a drawer by the
major-general who ordered it, Sir Charles Napier; it came to
light only after Napier moved on to a new post, and it fell
into the hands of his successor. Burton's superiors were
horrified that an officer and a gentleman could set down
such scabrous details with no sign of disapproval – this,
after all, was the age of Victoria and Albert – and his hopes
of promotion evaporated. After being deemed unsuitable
for the Mooltan campaign, he succumbed to a bout of fever,
and was shipped back to England on a stretcher.

It was all thoroughly typical of the bad luck that dogged
Burton for the rest of his life, and that seemed to spring
from something in his personality. His immense natural
vitality made him contemptuous of lesser men, and instead
of recognizing the problem and adjusting sensibly, he
exploded into rage and denunciatiom He was like an
untamed horse that cannot understand why it is not
selected for royal parades.

Back in Europe, he went to visit his family in Boulogne,

Sir Richard Burton, famous English traveller and scholar

and wrote four books about India – books full of fascinating material, but which reveal that fatal lack of self-discipline that was the root of his problems. He also planned expeditions to remote parts of the world – China, Tibet, South America, Africa – and, by way of diversion, danced with the plump and pretty Isabel Arundell, without suspecting for a moment that she was his destiny as he was hers.

At the time he met her, his mind was on his boldest and most dangerous venture so far: to pass himself off as an Arab in order to make the pilgrimage to Mecca. The Royal Geographical Society agreed to finance the expedition, and Burton decided to accustom himself to his new identity while still in London. Like Sherlock Holmes, he assumed his disguise and melted into the London fog. In effect, he became a Moslem; this was no charade, for Burton regarded all religions as holy, and greatly preferred Islam to Christianity. In 1853 he set out for Arabia disguised as a Pathan, an Afghanistan Moslem, and in this guise travelled to Cairo, Suez, Medina and – finally – Mecca. The book he wrote on his return a year later – *Pilgrimage to El-Medinah and Mecca* – brought him instant fame.

During this time Isabel had prayed for his safety and schemed how to meet him when he returned. She was not in the least surprised when he became a household name – she had always known he was a giant among men. But she was still no nearer her goal of making him her husband. Here in London, life was stiflingly genteel, and out there, her Richard was risking his life among savages. She needed all her self-control to suppress her frustration.

She needed even more when she learned that he was off on another dangerous expedition – this time to another Moslem holy city that forbade infidels: Harar in Abyssinian Somaliland. It was the centre of the slave trade in eastern Africa, which may be one reason why no white man had ever entered it and lived. Again disguised as an Arab, Burton gained entry to the citadel and was received by the emir, after which he joined his two British companions, Speke and Stroyan, outside the walls. But their camp was ambushed by 350 savage Somali warriors, and in the battle that ensued, Stroyan was killed and Burton received lance wounds in his cheeks that scarred him for life. When he returned to England his success was overshadowed by this incident. He was once more under a cloud.

In a few months, after writing up his experiences and urging the government to suppress slavery, Burton flung himself into action again and went off to fight in the Crimean War. Isabel had lost the chance to meet him yet again. She tried to force herself upon Florence Nightingale as a means of reaching the front, but Miss Nightingale regretted that she was too young and inexperienced. This was particularly frustrating, since many women with no taste for adventure were allowed to follow the British forces. Instead, Isabel directed her energies into a vigorous campaign of social work among the fallen women of East London. She was now twenty-five, and still a spinster. Tales of Burton's exploits among the harems of the Bosphorus reached London and depressed her spirits still further.

Then, on the racecourse at Ascot in June 1856, she recognized a familiar face in the crowd. It was her Romany prophetess, Hagar Burton. 'Well, are you Isabel Burton yet?' Isabel shook her head gloomily. 'Patience! It is just coming,' called Hagar, waving as the crowds separated them.

She was right. That August, Isabel and her sister were walking in the Botanical Gardens at Kew when they met Burton. He recognized them on sight and they stopped to talk. From then on for Isabel it was as if everything had fallen into place. For an intoxicating fortnight there were daily meetings. He discovered that she had read all his books and knew every step of his travels. With Burton thinking himself the pursuer and Isabel intent on capturing him, the result was inevitable. Burton proposed. 'But don't give me your answer now, because it will mean a very big step for you – no less than giving up your people and all that you are used to.' Isabel remained silent, struck dumb with relief. Burton interpreted her hesitation as indecision and said remorsefully, 'Forgive me; I ought not to have asked so much.' At which Isabel jerked herself out of her trance of ecstasy. 'I don't want to think it over! I've been thinking it over for five years. I would rather have a crust and a tent with you than be queen of all the world . . . Yes, yes, YES!'

But there were still – as Hagar's prophecy had foretold many problems to overcome. Burton visited the Arundell home – not as a suitor, but as an aquaintance of the sisters – but failed to impress Mrs Arundell, who found him appalling beyond belief: an atheist, an adventurer, and far too obviously a man of the world. It would probably have given her a heart attack to realize that Isabel intended to marry him, but she was spared this insight.

Now securely in possession of the man of her destiny, Isabel's only nagging anxiety was that he seemed to be insufficiently religious. True, he was interested in religion; he had been initiated into the Hindu, Muslim, Protestant, Catholic and Sikh faiths; but that was not quite the same thing. He explained disarmingly that he thought Catholicism 'a terrible religion for a man of the world to live in, but a good one to die in'. She would have to work on him. Isabel's own faith, though ardent, was hardly orthodox – it involved belief in magic, spirits and the prophetic power of dreams. One night she dreamed Richard came to her to say goodbye. The next morning she found a letter waiting at the breakfast table: he had left on another expedition, this time to find the source of the Nile. He hated emotional farewells.

During the next two years she heard nothing from him; but she was sustained by Hagar Burton's prophecy and the occasional newspaper report. She worried constantly about him and found some relief in prayer. It was a bitter-sweet pleasure to hear him discussed among her social set, and she caused mild astonishment by defending him vehemently if he was criticized. During 1857, on a tour of Europe with her sister and brother-in-law, she found that every vista reminded her of Richard. 'I believe that we often meet in spirit, and often look at the same star.' In the meantime several less remarkable men did their best to gain her favour. In Geneva she was pursued by a wealthy American widower, and in Genoa, a Russian general, loaded with decorations and titles, managed to obtain the room next to hers, and bombarded her with flowers and violin serenades that began at six in the morning. But Isabel was not to be tempted. Instead she set out to toughen herself for life as an explorer's wife by hiking and mountaineering in thick boots, wearing red petticoats for safety (they could be seen easily at a distance).

In the African hinterland, Burton's expedition was hacking its way slowly through jungle and plodding through swamps and deserts. Eventually they found themselves on the shores of Lake Tanganyika, which Burton unhesitatingly declared to be the source of the Nile. While he gathered information and wrote up his notes, he sent his companion Speke to explore to the north. As a result, Speke discovered Lake Victoria, and proclaimed this the source of the Nile. (He later proved to be correct.) The dispute became acrimonious, and after nursing him through a bout of fever, Burton suggested that Speke would return to England – having obtained his promise not to announce their discoveries until Burton returned. As soon as he returned Speke forgot his promise, described their discoveries to the Royal Geographical Society and basked in the fame that he should have been sharing with Burton. He even persuaded the Royal Geographical Society to make him the head of a new expedition – which would not include Burton. When Burton finally returned he was hardly noticed. (He was to have his revenge later when Speke committed suicide just before he was due to confront Burton in a debate.)

The day after he landed in England Burton stopped at the house of a friend to enquire about Isabel's whereabouts; by one of those remarkable coincidences that seem to punctuate their love story, he found her there seeking news of him. They rushed out of the house, hailed a cab and, for the next hour or so, drove around London in one another's arms.

Burton was much changed by the hardships of the African journey. Twenty-one bouts of fever had reduced him to 'a mere skeleton, with brown skin hanging in bags, his eyes protruding, and his lips drawn away from his teeth'. Isabel was now in her element; she wanted nothing more than to nurse the man she adored. 'I sit and look at him and think: You are mine, and there is no man on earth the least like you.' Mrs Arundell was less enthusiastic. Now she had no doubt of Isabel's intentions, she opposed them with the fervour of an ardent Christian defying the Devil. Isobel must be mad if she thought her parents would ever consent to her marrying a penniless atheist.

As unyielding as her mother, Isabel wrote her a long letter spelling out Burton's wonderful qualities, and concluding: 'I wish I were a man. If I were I would be Richard Burton; but being only a woman, I would be Richard Burton's wife.' Mrs Arundell was totally unmoved – Burton had remarked that both mother and daughter were 'gifted with the noble firmness of mules'. Meanwhile, he was planning another expedition – this time to pursue yet another of his dubious anthropological interests: polygamy. Isabel, now virtually telepathic where Burton was concerned, was talking with friends when she burst out: 'I am not going to see Richard for some time.' Soon afterwards a note arrived from Burton in which he explained why he was leaving for America, and expressing the hope that when he returned she would have made up her mind.

For the next nine months, while Burton interviewed Mormons in Salt Lake City, and discussed scalping techniques with Red Indians, Isabel devoted her energies to learning things that she thought might be useful for her life as the wife of an explorer: fishing, milking cows, grooming horses and riding astride them, rearing poultry, planting vegetables and learning how to cook, ironing laundry, and even practising the art of swordsmanship ('so I can defend Richard if he is attacked,' she explained to the quizzical fencing master).

Burton was a hopeless correspondent, and Isabel had to rely on telepathy and newspaper reports to learn his whereabouts. During Christmas 1860, in the depths of the Yorkshire dales, Isabel saw a paragraph in *The Times* announcing that Richard was back. Sending herself a telegram, she escaped the family gathering and after travelling nine miles in a blizzard, caught the first train to London. Shortly afterwards she and Burton were secretly married in a Catholic ceremony. Burton, who regarded weddings as 'barbarous and indelicate exhibitions', was embarrassed and annoyed at being pointed out as a bridegroom, and whispered to Isabel to pretend they'd been married a couple of years. Isabel happily agreed, as she would have agreed if he had suggested breaking the ice and jumping into the Serpentine. Nothing mattered except that, after ten years of waiting, she was Mrs Richard Burton.

A few days after the marriage, two of Isabel's aunts saw

her entering what they took to be bachelor's quarters and rushed to report the scandal to her parents. But by this time they already knew, and even Mrs Arundell finally overcame her objections and learned to accept her famous son-in-law. Her change of heart may have been connected with the fact that he now had a 'regular job' – a posting as British Consul on the remote and fever-infested island of Fernando Po off the coast of West Africa, known in the diplomatic service as 'the Foreign Office Grave'. Unfortunately, conditions there were so appalling that no white woman could hope to survive them; so once again, Isabel had to accept separation. As they parted, Burton for once allowed his emotions to show; seven months of marriage to Isabel had made him aware how much he loved her. During the next two years they managed only a handful of meetings.

Now living again with her parents, Isabel was kept busy with the task of editing Burton's latest book defending polygamy; she took care to add an introductory note explaining that the author did not practise it. In fact, she was less confident than she sounded. From 6,000 miles away, Burton reported with enthusiasm on the female warriors of Dahomey, and recommended the idea of women as soldiers for the attention of the British War Office. As far as he could see, its only disadvantage was that 'wherever she-soldiery is, celibacy must be one of its rules, or the troops will be in a state of chronic disorder between the ages of fifteen and thirty-five'. He went on to say that the king of Dahomey had had to delay an impending battle on finding that 150 of his warriors were pregnant, 'so difficult is chastity in the tropics'. For Isabel this comment was the last straw. She stormed into the Foreign Office in tears and begged for Burton's transfer to a more suitable post where they could be together. Swayed as much by Isabel's influential relatives as by the unpalatability of Burton's unorthodox Government Reports (which tended to concentrate on matters of anthropological interest such as aphrodisiacs, calamities, prostitution and decapitation dances) the Foreign Office agreed. Burton was appointed to Santos, in Brazil.

Faced at last with the exotic climes she had dreamed about, Isabel at first found it disappointingly unromantic. As three-inch cockroaches seethed about their room, Burton growled, 'I suppose you think you look very pretty standing on a chair and howling at those innocent creatures?' With characteristic determination she pulled herself together, climbed down and set to work with a slipper; in two hours she'd bagged ninety-seven.

There were even worse things to contend with: the consulate at Santos was surrounded by mangrove swamps; there were spiders as big as crabs; and terrible diseases. She soon caught cholera and was covered with boils (which she combated by drinking stout). All around was a steamy, brilliant landscape, brightly coloured birds and flowers shining out from the rich green jungle. Local society was dissolute, smoking huge cigars and drinking brandy for breakfast. Slaves and animals were kept in conditions of utmost squalor.

But Isabel was determined to cope, and she quickly set about making a home for them in an old convent. She unpacked the fifty-seven trunks she had brought from England, and within a few weeks was organizing her first dinner party. The household grew rapidly, consisting of a large number of servants and hired slaves, whom she treated kindly and assisted with religious instruction and medical care. There was also a huge menagerie of sick and needy animals upon whom she lavished affection. Her personal servant and particular pet was a negro dwarf called Chico. Isabel described him as 'brimming full of intelligence', and thought that 'there is in him something superior and refined . . .' She surmounted the inevitable setbacks (such as finding Chico trying to roast her favourite cat over the kitchen fire), but was disappointed to find that Burton had very little interest in their home.

Within a month of their arrival he was off to explore the interior. For a man with his broad interests Brazil and the surrounding countries were an endless source of fascinating information. He sent home reports on mineral resources, botany, zoology and unusual local customs. Fortunately Isabel was on hand to write up and edit the reports that went to London. Most of the time things went smoothly, and the fact that the British Consul was usually absent went unnoticed in faraway Whitehall.

After three years they were both worn out with the climate and the inevitable illnesses. Burton, now drinking heavily, swore that he would resign. At this, Isabel returned to London and once again used her influence (and tenacity) to secure the post they'd always dreamed of: Damascus. At last she would see Tancred's Mysterious East.

Burton was certainly qualified for the position; he was the foremost orientalist of his day, fluent in Arabic, a Moslem initiate, who understood both the people and the country. In practice, however, this was not necessarily what the British government wanted. Their aim was to maintain a peaceful status quo, something Burton was entirely unqualified to do. The Turkish viceroy – or pasha – of Syria was a shrewd and exceptionally corrupt man; he eyed Burton with suspicion from the first, realizing that unlike his predecessor and colleagues, this was a man who would understand exactly what was going on in the Pashalik, and who would be unable to resist the temptation to try and improve things.

But for the moment all went well enough. Burton arrived before Isabel, and plunged into work with relief and enthusiasm. He felt reborn; he was in the East that he adored and to which he fundamentally belonged. He had scarcely arrived in Damascus when he set out to climb the nearest mountain. Six weeks later he was off into the eastern desert studying archaeological sites. The pasha regarded all this with suspicion; for him, it was inexplicable that a foreign official should go wandering about the desert and mountains to look at old ruins; Burton was obviously on some secret diplomatic mission, and probably plotting with the tribesmen . . .

Isabel arrived with her English maid, five dogs (including a St Bernard), and a mountain of baggage; she was expecting to stay about ten years. A lovely house on a hill outside the city was selected, and was soon filled with a troublesome Arab staff, and an enormous collection of unsuitable pets, ranging from leopards to lambs, whose numbers were only kept in check by their tendency to eat one another. Mostly, Burton ignored the domestic turmoil, only shaking his head over Isabel's incorrigible passion for nursing the poor and sick with her experimental draughts which, together with her eagerness to baptize the sick and dying into the Catholic faith aroused a certain amount of adverse comment in the foreign community.

But it was Burton's conduct that caused the problems – not that there was anything wrong with it, for he was scrupulously fair, honest and conscientious. And that was precisely what upset his critics. Surrounded by the kind of bribery and corruption the Arabs took for granted, he was rigidly incorruptible. When emissaries of the pasha presented themselves with a large bribe, he flew into a rage and threw them out bodily. Moreover, he refused to mind his own business. He was outraged by the extortionate rates of interest charged by Jewish moneylenders, and sent unfavourable reports back to London. He obviously preferred Moslems to Christians, and stuck up for them against his fellow countrymen – an unforgivable sin in a

Richard and Isabel Burton

When Isabel and Richard Burton were living in
Damascus, they kept open house once a week.
Every race and creed were welcome and the
atmosphere was generally genial. However, Isabel's
occasional desire to instil European habits into her
guests sometimes went wrong: on one occasion
when an Arab noblemen called, she decided to
place his wives in chairs and expected the husband
to pass them cakes or cups of coffee, thereby
breaking every sacred tradition of the Islamic
home. The angry guest stormed out, saying 'pray
don't teach our women what they do not know'
followed by his scuttling ladies.

British consul. But he also alienated the Moslems by fining
a Druse tribe for attacking two English missionaries. He
angered the Greeks by protesting when their bishop seized
a Jewish synagogue and cemetery. For all his remarkable
qualities as a human being, Burton had what one
biographer calls 'a curious ability to do the right thing in the
wrong way'.

Perhaps his greatest mistake concerned a Moslem
mystical sect called the Shazlis. For all his professed
agnosticism, Burton was deeply interested in mysticism,
and attended some of the Shazli religious ceremonies in
disguise. One day, a Shazli in a state of ecstasy saw a vision
of a man who commanded those who sought true salvation
to follow him to heaven. When he decided that the man in
the vision was a Spanish monk who happened to be Isabel's
father confessor, the Shazlis prepared to accept
Christianity. Isabel immediately agreed to sponsor them –
all 2,000 – and Burton was so impressed by this mass

conversion that he wrote to the Foreign Office proposing that the British government should purchase a tract of land for them. Meanwhile the pasha, concerned that this defection from Islam might spread, arrested large numbers of Shazlis and seized their property. Burton raged, and threatened reprisals in the name of the British government. His Jewish and Christian enemies saw an opportunity to get rid of him, and deluged the Foreign Office with complaints.

As far as the British government was concerned, this was the last straw. The Foreign Office decided Burton had to go. In August 1871, after a mere two years in Damascus, he was recalled unceremoniously. The Burtons were in their summer quarters at Bludan, in Lebanon, when he received a letter from the Beirut vice consul telling him that he had been replaced. He galloped off to Damascus, then sent Isabel a brief message that read: 'I am superseded. Pay, pack and follow.' Without looking back, he left for London.

That was typical of Burton; he found fools so irritating that his reaction to injustice was to shrug his shoulders and brood in silence. Like a jilted lover, he refused even to think about his betrayal. It was Isabel who was left to write indignant letters to the Foreign Office and – finally – a book about the whole affair:

Back in London, she confronted Lord Granville – who was responsible for Burton's dismissal – and forced him to give her an official statement explaining his reasons. There was an outcry in *The Times*, and the Foreign Office felt compelled to publish its own side of the story. Left to himself, Burton would merely have sunk into gloomy disgust – and probably alcoholism. Isobel preferred stirring up hornets' nests. Her campaign was so successful that Lord Granville eventually wrote to ask her if her husband would accept the consulship of Trieste, whose last occupant had been the amiable Irish novelist Charles Lever.

Richard and Isabel Burton

Typically, Burton was ungrateful. He would have preferred Bombay or Peking. But since beggars cannot be choosers, and since by this time the improvident Burtons were almost literally beggars, there was nothing for it but to accept.

Isabel loved Trieste; Burton hated it – although he eventually came to tolerate it. They moved into a top-floor apartment with twenty-six rooms and a magnificent view. The salary was only £700 a year, but living was cheap, and Burton supplemented his income with a steady stream of books: travel books, history books (one on swords), archaeological studies, poetry, translations of classics of near-pornography like the *Pentameron of Catherine of Navarre* and the *Kama Sutra* (like his friend Swinburne he loved nothing so much as shocking the Victorians), and even a *History of Farting*, which he took care to place on the table when Isabel was giving a tea party.

Isabel herself enjoyed some literary success with her *Inner Life of Syria*, and on the strength of the royalties, Richard agreed to take her to India. They travelled via Arabia, and travelled from Jeddah on a ship full of Moslem pilgrims packed like sardines, where Isabel's nursing skills were urgently needed. The voyage was grim (although the Burtons travelled first class), but when Isabel arrived in India, she knew it had been worth it. This was truly the very essence of the East that she had dreamed about since reading *Tancred*. With Burton as her guide she saw the sights, rode on elephants, haunted the bazaars, climbed the hills. But when they returned to Trieste, Burton knew instinctively that this sentimental journey was also a leave-taking.

Life in Trieste might have been idyllic if Burton had not been such a pessimistic fatalist; they were not badly off, and HM Government seemed to have no objection to their endless travels to Italy, Austria, London, even the Middle

East. But Burton somehow felt that he had missed the crock of gold at the end of the rainbow. He was pointlessly embittered and thought of himself as ill-done-to. There was some truth in it – but then, it might have been worse, far worse.

After 1883, things suddenly improved – financially at least. For years Burton had worked on his translation of the *Arabian Nights* – as much out of nostalgia for the East as a desire to give the world another version. He decided to bring out a privately printed edition, with copious notes. A publisher offered him £500 for the rights but Isabel refused. Instead, she personally mailed out 34,000 circulars. Unexpectedly, the ten-volume edition became a best-seller, and made Burton 16,000 guineas (£16,800), a vast fortune at that time. (To translate into modern money it should be multiplied at least fifty times.) Burton remarked cynically that now he knew the tastes of England, they need never be without money.

Although Isabel was only in her mid-fifties, and Burton in his mid-sixties; both felt themselves to be in failing health. When Isabel was told that she had a cancerous growth that might be arrested by an immediate operation, she rejected the idea because it would worry Richard; in effect, she decided to accept a form of slow suicide. In 1886, both were delighted to receive a telegram from the Queen conferring a knighthood on Burton – Isabel felt that it was as much in recoguition of her role as a wife as Burton's as a public servant, for the Queen regarded the memory of her departed Albert with the same reverence Isabel felt for Richard.

Now her chief concern was to save her husband's soul by converting him to Catholicism. Convinced that the Moslem and Christian paradises were located in completely different parts of Heaven, she was afraid that they would fail to meet in the hereafter if he died a Moslem. Burton gave way to the extent of praying with her regularly, but nothing could persuade him to renounce his intellectual independence and his ironical attitude towards Christians.

Finally, Burton's health gave them such cause for concern that they decided to spend some of their newly acquired fortune on a personal physician. Burton was subject to sudden fits of paralysis and gout. As improvident as ever, the trio travelled around Europe. Burton still dreamed of a final posting in the East, but Isabel – and the doctor – knew better.

In mid October 1890, Burton told her that a bird had been tapping on his window all morning, and that he regarded this as a bad omen; when she pointed out that he often fed the birds, Burton said: 'It was not that window.' Three days later, on 19 October, he woke up in the night complaining of gout; a few hours later he was finding it difficult to breathe. Isabel sent for a priest, but Burton died at dawn, before he arrived. Isabel refused to believe that he was dead, and with some difficulty, persuaded the priest to administer extreme unction anyway. Then she sat by the body all day, hoping that he would revive, and later expressed her conviction that his soul had 'gone forth with the setting sun'.

Burton was given a magnificent funeral by the Bishop of Trieste, with a pomp and ceremony that he would have hated. There were three memorial services, and 1,000 masses said for the repose of his spirit – to the disgust of Burton's family, who felt that the Catholic Church, of which they disapproved, had hijacked Burton's immortal soul. His sister, Lady Stisted, had some extremely unkind things to say about it in her biography of her brother.

The British public was even more outraged when it was revealed that Isabel had burned most of her husband's papers, including the diary he had kept throughout his adult life. The Victorians could understand the kind of prudery that might lead her to burn his translations of 'pornography' like *The Perfumed Garden*, but surely even a wife had no right to destroy important biographical material of one of England's greatest travel writers? There was a great deal of acrimonious correspondence in *The Times*.

Isabel was past caring. With her husband dead, she felt that her own life was over. It made no difference to her that she had cancer – it merely meant that she would be reunited with Richard sooner.

Of the profits from the *Arabian Nights*, there were less than four florins left at the time of his death, and Isabel dropped these in the poor box. As the wife of a government official, she was later granted a pension of £150 a year. But she turned down an offer of a tomb in Westminster Abbey, since Burton's name would merely be listed among other explorers, like Speke and Livingstone. In any case, she and Richard had already chosen the site of his tomb – in the Mortlake Catholic Cemetery. Burton had told her that he wanted to be buried in an Arab tent, and Isabel raised the money for it by subscription – an Arab tent in marble, complete with tinkling camel bells. In the six years she had remaining to her after Burton's death, she wrote an enormous Life, and issued a memorial edition of his works. She even supervised the waxwork of him – in Arab dress – in Madame Tussaud's. And on Passion Sunday, 21 March, 1896 she died, and was buried beside him in the Arab tent at Mortlake.

Chapter Eight

Elizabeth Barrett and Robert Browning

It was not until 1935, when Rudolf Bessier's play *The Barretts of Wimpole Street* became the hit of both the London and the New York theatre season, that Robert Browning and Elizabeth Barrett took their place in the ranks of the world's great lovers.

It was certainly the last thing in the world that Elizabeth expected. In 1845, she was thirty-nine years old, and had been an invalid for six years. She wrote poetry, which brought her a certain fame, but was reconciled to the idea of living the rest of her life in her sickroom at 50 Wimpole Street. Small and delicate, with dark eyes, a large, well-shaped mouth, her pale face framed in ringlets, she spent her days lying on her sofa, or sitting at the table writing letters to her innumerable correspondents.

Every night, her father – whose bedroom adjoined hers – came through the connecting door, took her hand in both of his, and said spontaneous prayers. Edward Moulton Barrett was a typical Victorian tyrant who brooked no disagreement or contradiction. Stern and pious, he had always imposed strict discipline on his wife and family; her death did not soften his attitude, and it removed the one tender and sympathetic audience for the Barrett children. Yet to Elizabeth he could be kind and affectionate. She was loyal and dutiful and from an early age had a quiet seriousness of mind which sustained him. She was also helpless and never challenged his authority, unlike the others who had to be continually reminded of their duty.

Elizabeth's happy childhood years before her illness had been spent in the countryside of the Malvern Hills, living in a house called 'Hope End' (named by Mr Barrett with no trace of humour). After the death of Mrs Barrett the family moved several times. In 1840 they were living in Torquay when a second tragedy struck: Elizabeth's eldest brother Edward was drowned. Her delicate health was greatly undermined by her terrible sense of loss. Soon after this disaster they moved to 50 Wimpole Street in London, and she had developed an almost morbid fear of meeting anyone outside her family and a close circle of friends. Only 'Flush' her young Cavalier spaniel and constant companion, with puppy-like high spirits, enlivened this restricted existence.

But Elizabeth was also deeply fond of her family and acted as buffer between her brothers and sisters and their difficult father. She could often intercede on their behalf to bring about some small change in the rigid household routine; perhaps a tactful friend might be allowed to call for tea. Although all now grown up, Elizabeth and her brothers and sisters were treated by their father as children and he would not allow any of them to marry. This did not much affect Elizabeth who regarded herself as an invalid and now too old for marriage anyway, or her sister Arabel who was quietly resigned to a pious life as a spinster, but was very hard on the youngest sister Henrietta who was young and vivacious. Elizabeth's five brothers were similarly ruled by the domestic tyrant whose financial control of their lives prevented escape.

It was into this strange detached life that Robert Browning burst on a cold January day in 1845. 'I love your verses with all my heart Miss Barrett' – thus began her impetuous correspondent who went on to praise 'this great

Elizabeth Barrett and Robert Browning

Elizabeth Barrett Browning

living poetry of yours . . . I do, as I say, love these books
with all my heart – and I love you too.'

They had never met, but she knew and admired his
poetry and so as she read on felt she already knew him. She
wrote back thanking him for his interest in her *work* and
went on to discuss writing as one poet to another. And so
began a unique correspondence which over a period of
nearly two years reveals the development of a rare and
complete relationship.

Robert Browning's life was as carefree as Elizabeth's was
confined. Six years her junior, he lived at home with
indulgent parents and a devoted only sister in Camberwell.
Like Elizabeth he was largely self-taught, reading widely in
his scholarly father's extensive library. He was well read in
French, Italian, Greek and Spanish literature, and was able
to live on the modest income from his plays and poetry. A
lively and sociable creature, he was well liked, spending
much time dining out with friends and going to the opera
or theatre. At thirty-three, he was a handsome, distinctive
man, with fine, clear-cut features framed in dark whiskers,
which were as fashionable as his lemon-coloured gloves.
He had travelled abroad, to Moscow, as secretary to the
Russian ambassador and had twice been to Italy – a country
he loved.

It was on his return from Italy in 1844 that he came across
Miss Barrett's newly published poems. Reading them he
found himself deeply moved; he empathized totally with
the spirit and intellect of the writer. He loved 'the fresh
strange music, the affluent language, the exquisite pathos
and true and brave thought'. He sensed behind the words
the presence of a vision close to his own, and longed to meet
her. They had a mutual friend, Mr Kenyon, and Browning
questioned him closely for every detail about Miss Barrett.
He was told that she had not long to live; she spent her days
in a heavily curtained room. Her home life was dismal, she

and her numerous grown-up brothers and sisters were dominated by their tyrannical father who discouraged visitors. Not to be put off, Browning one day accompanied Mr Kenyon to the Barrett family home, but they had to leave without seeing Miss Barrett; she was unwell.

Now, he wrote that first letter, hoping she would permit a meeting. But her reply held him away: 'Winters shut me up as they do a dormouse's eyes . . . in the Spring we shall see.' They found a great deal in common and exchanged letters every day or so; then, when the first warm weather arrived Browning again asked if he might visit but she remained elusive: 'little later comes my Spring'.

At the end of May they finally met. He saw for the first time the 'small delicate figure which did not rise from the sofa, pale ringletted face, great eager, wistfully pathetic eyes'. They already knew one another from their letters; now this meeting confirmed in Browning all of the attraction he had previously felt only for her spirit. Of this first meeting she later wrote: 'when you came, you never went away.'

They met on Tuesday; on Thursday he wrote the only letter of their correspondence which has been destroyed. He rashly told her that he had fallen in love with her. She read it in agitation; whatever her feelings, she did not feel able to encourage such impetuous declarations. She spent a sleepless night and then returning his letter, wrote forbidding all further expressions of love; but the tone was friendly and she ended by inviting him to call again whenever he wished. He came back again a day or so later, sensibly resolved to accept whatever terms she imposed.

The visits and the letters continued regularly. They discussed the work of Tennyson, the novels of George Sand, they corrected one another's manuscripts; he told her about the beautiful scenery of Italy and they agreed that this must be a wonderful place to settle down. Flush sensed

> A lover . . . tries to stand in well with the pet dog
> of the house.
>
> *Molière*

the growing intimacy between his mistress and this enthusiastic visitor. He eyed Browning with suspicion and whenever possible attacked his umbrella (living in hope of one day reaching a leg). But Browning with typical good humour, managed to soothe the dog's temper with cakes.

On 14 June, Browning enclosed a yellow rose in his letter; and then all summer long flowers arrived bringing scent and colour into the dull city room. She always saw him alone. On the days when he was absent his letters came. And when he himself was gone, his flowers were there. His presence gave her strength and a new determination, and by midsummer she was venturing outside to take the air – 'I am really alive after it!' But after such a long surrender to invalidism she felt 'no better than a tired bird'.

At about this time her doctor suggested that since there were encouraging signs of improvement, Miss Barrett might benefit from spending the next winter in some warmer climate, perhaps Malta or Alexandria. She hoped and planned for such a trip; one of her brothers and her sister Arabel offered to accornpany her. But at the last moment her father came down against the plan. After years of encouraging her to think of herself as frail and sick, he now declared there was nothing wrong with her but 'obstinacy and dry toast'. Unlike her brothers and sisters, Elizabeth was not dependent on her father's financial support, she had a small income of her own left to her by an uncle – but although she was now in her fortieth year, she still felt herself bound to obey his wishes. But it now began to dawn on her that the paternal love in which she had trusted was motivated by selfishness and possessiveness.

When Browning came to see her on 25 August Elizabeth poured out her disappointment, speaking bluntly about the domestic problems caused by her father's autocratic temper. Her cheerful polka-loving sister Henrietta had recently been forbidden to accept a proposal of marriage from a devoted admirer named Captain Surtees Cook. The scenes which followed had distressed them all terribly; poor Henrietta had finally been forced to promise she would never see him again.

From this time onwards, Elizabeth's letters are full of confidences; a new trust had developed between them. She wrote to him of her most sacred memories, of her past life and of her brother's death. Deeply moved, Browning wanted to repay confidence with confidence, but it was only three months since she had forbidden him to express intimate feelings. He hesitated before replying to her letter, and in those two days, Elizabeth began to worry. Was he unwell? Had she displeased him? She wrote on 30 August a letter asking 'the alms of just one line' to relieve her of her fears.

The appeal swept away all his doubts and he replied calmly and decisively: he loved her and he wanted to marry her. She replied with caution that she could not allow him 'to empty his water gourds into the sand'. Her paramount fear was that her invalidism might ruin his life. But she did not deny that she loved him. For Browning that was enough; now he felt certain of her he did not press her further. She could judge when the time was right. From this point on their correspondence took on the tone of an engaged couple and her letters answered his with endearments. He even called her by her family nickname: 'Ba'.

Although she now returned his love completely and openly, the obstacles still seemed insurmountable. First,

Robert Browning was asked by his future wife Elizabeth Barrett what an exceptionally obscure passage in one of his poems meant. Having puzzled over the passage for some time, Browning gave up the struggle. 'Miss Barrett,' he said, 'when that passage was written only God and Robert Browning knew what it meant. Now only God knows.'

there was her physical weakness. With his encouragement she began to grow stronger. She now went downstairs unassisted and a little later, as her confidence grew, wrote to him describing walks in nearby Regent's Park with Flush. She still feared becoming a burden to him, but she was determined to stay alive. Browning had made her feel that she possessed a future.

Their worst fear was that their love would be discovered. If Mr Barrett found out, Robert's letters would be destroyed before they reached her and Browning himself would be forbidden to enter the house. As it was, his visits were only permitted because her father was so convinced that no man could fall in love with her; he believed that their friendship was purely a literary affair – (he referred to Browning as 'the pomegranate man' after his book of poems *The Bell and the Pomegranate*). Neither of them was secretive by nature and they found it a strain to conceal their feelings of excitement and happiness. Elizabeth had always been open and truthful with her father; but she was now in an impossible position. She could not give up Browning.

As the months went by and they talked over their plans, so the tension grew. Flush lost control and bit Browning, but was sternly reprimanded by Elizabeth and never did it again. All through the spring Elizabeth's health improved. With great patience, Browning refrained from putting pressure on her about the date of their marriage. But as summer advanced they realized it would have to be soon; another cold winter in London would set back her recovery. Then her father unwittingly forced them to act.

'This night an edict has gone out,' Elizabeth wrote in a panic on 10 September. The Wimpole Street house was to be redecorated and they were to move elsewhere for a month. 'If you go, our marriage will be impossible for another year,' wrote Robert instantly. 'We must be *married directly* and go to Italy. I will go for a licence today and we can be married on Saturday.'

Two days later Elizabeth left the house accompanied by her maid Lily Wilson. Halfway to their destination, Elizabeth felt faint and had to be revived with smelling salts from a nearby chemist's. At last they reached Marylebone Church where Robert was waiting. The ceremony took place in the presence of two witnesses, a cousin and Lily Wilson. Then husband and wife parted. On returning to the house Mrs Browning regretfully took off her wedding ring and hung it around her neck on a ribbon. Flight would have to wait until she had more strength.

Browning did not visit the house at Wimpole Street again. During the next week the upheaval of the household removals hid the activities of Elizabeth and her maid as they packed for their departure. The boxes were smuggled out of the house and sent on ahead. Elizabeth wrote a letter for her father trying to explain and asking for his forgiveness. She hoped that in time he would come to understand and accept her decision. Just a week after their marriage, the Brownings met in a nearby bookshop then, accompanied by Lily Wilson and Flush, they climbed into a cab and set out for sunshine and Italy.

The years that followed were as idyllic as they had

Robert Browning

Elizabeth Barrett and Robert Browning

hoped. They lived first in Pisa, then moved to Florence –
'Florence . . . the brilliant city which murmurs so of the
fountain of intellectual youth for ever and ever.' Elizabeth's
health, transformed by the sunshine and optimism, went on
improving, and in 1849 she gave birth to a boy they named
'Penini' (a child 'like a rose possessed by a fairy'). They
toured all over Italy, climbed in the hills and stayed in
secluded country inns. Lily Wilson married a handsome
Florentine who moved in with the family. Even Flush found
life greatly improved; each day he accompanied Browning
on a long walk and at other times was allowed to run freely
– there were no dog thieves or park wardens in Florence.

Both the poets continued to write – Browning compared
the joy of poetry to a swimmer's delight in the sea. One day,
Elizabeth slipped into his hand a sheaf of poems, the
Sonnets from the Portuguese. In these she charts the progress
of their relationship: the hesitant development of her love,
her unwillingness to involve him in the life of an invalid,
then, as she yields to her certainty of his love for her, the
nature of late-born happiness.

There were two visits to England, but Elizabeth never
again saw her father. He remained unforgiving until his
death, returning all her letters with the seals intact. She was,
he declared, as 'one dead' to him, and commented of her
marriage: 'My daughter should have been thinking of
another world.' But Elizabeth's brothers and sisters
welcomed her, and she went to stay with Henrietta who
had also broken from their father's grip and was now a
blissfully contented Mrs Surtees Cook.

The Brownings' life in Italy and their travels about the
Continent went on for the next sixteen years, and are
described in their diaries and letters. Then quite suddenly
on a June evening in 1861, an attack of bronchitis suddenly
became worse. A doctor was sent for. Browning held
Elizabeth against him. 'Then,' as he later wrote, 'always

smiling, happily, and with a face like a girl's, in a few minutes she died in my arms, her head on my cheek.'

Elizabeth Barrett Browning left behind an enduring testimony of her great love for her husband, who had opened up her life into such happiness:

> How do I love thee? Let me count the ways.
> I love thee to the depth and breadth and height
> My soul can reach, when feeling out of sight
> For the ends of Being and ideal Grace.
> I love thee to the level of every day's
> Most quiet need, by sun and candlelight.
> I love thee freely, as men strive for Right;
> I love thee purely, as they turn from Praise.
> I love thee with the Passion put to use
> In my old griefs, and with my childhood's faith.
> I love thee with a love I seemed to lose
> With my lost saints, – I love thee with the breath,
> Smiles, tears, of all my life! – and, if God choose,
> I shall but love thee better after death.

Chapter Nine

Karen Blixen

When the film *Out of Africa* came out in 1986 a huge audience became aware of a love story which had until then remained virtually unknown: the affair between Karen Blixen and Denys Finch Hatton, the greatest of the white hunters and early conservationists, who was killed when his plane crashed in 1931.

Karen Blixen was born in Rungsted, Denmark in 1885. Her parents were respectably middle class, and lived comfortably on a small farming estate near Copenhagen. It was a dull, orderly life entirely dominated by women. Karen's father had died when she was ten and she felt his loss very acutely. He was an adventurous man, a hunter and a soldier, who loved nature and solitude. In his youth he had broken free from his narrow Danish background, after a beautiful cousin with whom he was in love died of typhoid. For several years he lived the life of a trapper with American Indians in the Wisconsin woods. When he returned to Denmark and settled down to family life with Karen's mother, he wrote books on his hunting experiences and became involved in politics. But he was at heart a deeply sensitive, melancholy man, and it was not until years after his death that Karen learned that he had hanged himself because he believed he had an incurable illness.

Karen was much like him – she shared his love of nature and books, and would always be attracted to wild places, and to simple 'uncivilized' people.

As a young woman, she found life in Denmark oppressive. The house, filled with her aunts and unmarried sisters,

had the atmosphere of a convent: '. . . it had the same feeling
. . . that one encounters . . . in a crowded compartment or
waiting room, where the windows are kept closed: the air
has been consumed.' She fought to keep her vitality, her
secret self, intact from their intrusion by writing plays and
learning to paint. At eighteen she persuaded her reluctant
family to let her attend the Royal Academy of Art in
Copenhagen, and in the following years studied art in Paris
and Rome. She was always dreaming of permanent escape;
but the opportunity eluded her until she was nearing the
end of her twenties.

She had been strongly attracted to her aristocratic second
cousin Hans, but he was indifferent to her, and in 1912, she
became engaged to his twin brother Bror, who had pursued
her with all the enthusiasm lacking in his brother. Bror
inherited the title of Baron von Blixen, but the family were
no longer wealthy and he worked running the dairy farm
on their estate. At first Karen had resisted Bror's advances
telling him that she could not face living in Denmark –
which she felt was the most oppressively provincial spot on
earth; it was not until they hit upon the idea of emigrating
that she accepted his proposal. They each had something
the other wanted, Bror had a title and an adventurous spirit,
but no money; Karen had family money and wanted
adventure. Many people were surprised at the match, for
the two seemed to have nothing in common. Her mother
had opposed the marriage, aware that Karen did not love
him. But in fact, with Bror's title and connections and
Karen's family money, the couple were, for the moment at
least, happily united in their eagerness to leave Denmark.

At this time, Karen was tall and slim, with long dark hair
usually pinned up into a bun under her wide-brimmed hat
with a veil. She had fine features, a slightly pointed chin,
longish nose and large very striking, dark eyes. Bror, two
years younger than Karen, was well built, with a cheerful

confident manner; he had short blondish hair and very blue
eyes, a well-suntanned face with rounded cheeks and full
generous lips. Their temperaments were totally different.
Bror had been brought up on horse racing, hunting, fishing,
fast cars, wild parties and the social pleasures of the Danish
aristocracy. He was an enthusiastic sportsman; robust and
outgoing, his sole purpose was to have a good time.
Irresponsible and generous, he had quickly made his way
through his inheritance. He was hopelessly unreliable,
especially in money matters, but nonetheless immensely
popular, even with those who lent him money. By contrast,
Karen was intense and intellectual. She read widely, spoke
several languages and was an accomplished painter.

In 1912, Bror (better known as Blix) went out to Kenya
and bought a large farm in the Ngong hills to the west of
Nairobi. The money was provided by Karen's family, who
were to be shareholders in a coffee-growing venture. Six
months later, Karen sailed out to join him. The day after her
arrival in Mombasa they were married in the register office,
with the King of Sweden, who happened to be visiting, as a
witness.

Then they travelled slowly inland on the narrow-gauge
railway, through strange, wild country completely unlike
the pastureland in Denmark. After the lush tropical
vegetation of the coast lands, they crossed great grass
plains, 'dry and burnt, like the colours in pottery', scattered
with thorn trees and game. The light was brilliant and
relentless. The sky seemed vast; the views immensely wide:
'everything you saw made for greatness and freedom'. As
they began to climb the eastern escarpment of the Rift
Valley, the scene changed, becoming a rocky, lunar
landscape. Finally, after two days, they arrived in the green
and fertile highlands: the Ngong hills.

The farm was twelve miles outside Nairobi, 6,000 feet
above sea level. There were magnificent views in all

In 1909 Theodore Roosevelt and his son Kermit went on safari in East Africa. They took with them 265 African porters who carried everything required for comfort in the bush: from dining tables and chairs to bathtubs. The procession stretched for over a mile. The porters also carried four tons of salt with which to cure the skins and meat of the animals bagged by their employers.

In ten months the expedition shot over 500 animals of seventy species, including nine white rhinos (which at that time were on the verge of extinction). Of these, there were four cows and one calf.

With the justification that they were collecting specimens for the Smithsonian Museum, they also killed 5,000 mammals, 4,000 birds, 2,000 reptiles and 500 fish.

directions, especially to the south, where great herds of zebra and wildebeest moved about the grass plains as far as the horizon, where Kilimanjaro rose in the distance.

The farm was made up of 42,000 acres of wood and grasslands, surrounded by undulating hills. There was a sense of the wilderness everywhere; monkeys shrieked in the forest; on the slopes of the hills were buffalo, eland and rhino; elephants and giraffes flourished in the dry bush. Here, Karen felt 'Africa distilled up through six thousand feet, like the strong refined essence of a continent.'

From the beginning, she had an affinity with the landscape and with the African people, which made her determined to stay. At her new home she found 1,200 Africans assembled to greet her, and they let out a great roar of welcome as she approached. These were the Kikuyu 'squatters' who lived on the farm, working as farmhands part of the year. 'The Natives were Africa in flesh and blood . . . The tall extinct volcano, the broad mimosa trees, the elephant and the giraffe, were not more truly Africa than the Natives were – small figures in immense scenery . . . We ourselves in boots, and in our constant great hurry, often jar with the landscape. The Natives are in accordance with it.'

She now immersed herself in becoming a coffee grower. In those few months before the outbreak of the First World War she learned to farm and to live as a wife. She furnished the house with antiques, heavy crystal glasses and fine china shipped from Denmark. With the help of a large body of African staff, she landscaped a garden, while Blix cleared the farmland and planted coffee bushes. Later in the year they went on safari and she discovered the thrill of seeing wild animals close up, of tracking them and shooting to kill. Until then she had never slept in a tent, handled a rifle or killed anything. Hunting was a way of life at that time, when game was teeming everywhere. She understood the excitement of hunting, but later did little of it herself. 'Before I took over management of the farm, I had been keen on shooting. But when I became a farmer I put away my rifles.' Every day, she would ride out across the Massai grasslands on her horse Rouge, and absorb the strange new impressions of the country she had so wholeheartedly adopted.

There was also time to think, for there were many days and nights when she was left alone. Blix was often away on business in Nairobi, which at that time was a scruffy pioneer town that had grown haphazardly around the railhead. Its pot-holed mud streets divided rows of roughly built, tin-roofed buildings with raised wooden pavements, like a town in the Wild West. Blix described it as 'more like an empty old sardine tin than anything else'. Nonetheless, there were amusements to be found at the two hotels and the newly opened Muthaiga Club.

Most of the early pioneers were the younger sons of landed families, who found in Kenya large tracts of virgin territory at modest cost, abundant native labour and a sense of adventure. There was an atmosphere of eighteenth-century feudalism, and even a second son could own and run a large estate. But the risks and uncertainties of clearing the land and making a living were enormous. This fact determined the temperament – and class – of the early settlers; they tended to be strong-willed, energetic individuals, whose financial resources allowed them a certain freedom. They hurled themselves into recreation with the same energy with which they cleared the bush and hunted game. It was said that the exceptionally pure air in the highlands produced euphoria in white people, who were therefore not held strictly accountable for their actions. Kenya had a highly erotic atmosphere, civilized inhibitions were forgotten, and serial polygamy was athletically practised. In the bars of steamers women were accustomed to the famous question, 'are you married or do you live in Kenya?'

Karen did not mind being left alone; she had plenty to occupy her. She supervised the building of a coffee-roasting factory, and a school and clinic for the African community that lived on her land. Then, in 1914, when the war broke out, everyone in the colony was needed. Karen helped Blix transport supplies to the Tanzanian front, on the other side of the Massai land. On one occasion, when her convoy of cattle was attacked by lions, she chased them off single-handedly with a whip. In keeping with her surroundings, she had become tough and resourceful. However, in the following year, she found herself continually ill. At first malaria was diagnosed, but did not respond to treatment;

finally it was found that she had contracted syphilis from Blix. So in 1915, she went home to Denmark to receive the long and painful course of mercury treatment which was then the only cure available.

When she returned to the farm a year later the marriage was effectively over, though they continued to run the farm together. In her absence Blix had continued his indiscriminate affairs, drinking heavily and flinging wild parties; he had also run up huge debts (and for some time, even had to retire to a cave in the hills in order to avoid irate creditors, telling his staff to say he was 'on safari'). But for all his roguery, Blix was charming, kind, supportive and unrepentant; and he and Karen remained close friends and continued to appear in public as a couple.

Denys Finch Hatton entered Karen's life just at a time when she was most in need of a love affair to restore her battered pride and alleviate her loneliness.

They met on 5 April 1918, at a Muthaiga Club dinner. Rain drummed on the roof – the rainy season had begun – and the club was full of Chinese paper lanterns. (One biographer has pointed out most of the seduction scenes in her later work are accompanied by rain – or snow, or salt spray.) Karen was curious, having heard many admiring comments about Finch Hatton. He proved to be a tall, witty, lean, wry, balding, incredibly handsome aristocrat. He had been at Eton with the poet Julian Grenfell, was a friend of Rupert Brooke, and very much a part of that 'golden youth' generation. In 1918 he was thirty-one and, when Karen meet him, was on leave from the Mesopotamian front where he was a pilot. The second son of the Earl of Winchilsea, Denys had rejected the conventional life of his class in England and had come to Kenya eight years before, after leaving Oxford, announcing, 'England is so small, much too small.' He bought land in the north and had set up a string of trading posts. Like Karen, he had found the enormity and wildness of the African landscape inspirational. Freedom of time and space were essential conditions of his life. He was a quiet but oddly impressive man, and for Karen, his mysterious reserve – which contrasted so much with Blix's extrovert charm – heightened the magnetism.

Writing of Denys a friend later said, 'One got the impression that he could bring anything he undertook to a fortunate issue . . . I saw him first, fingering a pistol in a Nairobi gun shop . . . with the casual interest that men of action will show for such toys and well I liked the look of his scholarly appearance, which had also about it the suggestion of an adventurous wanderer . . .' He possessed an undefined assurance which throughout his life attracted respect and admiration. But there was also about him a certain aloofness, whose source lay in the fact that ever since boyhood he had been accustomed to a certain deference from the world, which meant that he had the deepest objection to being bored, exploited or possessed. He had been adored all his life, and there was a sense in which he wanted to escape and be left alone.

Denys was named after the god of wine, Dionysus, and he reminded Karen of a classical bronze statue. He had a magnificent physique, but more importantly for her, he was intelligent and sensitive, a man with whom she could share her thoughts and love of literature. The attraction was immediate and mutual. But for the moment, neither acknowledged it. In any case, he was not the sort of man to fall quickly in love.

Their next meeting was a month later. Denys was due to return to Egypt, and the Blixens invited him to join them and a small group of friends in a hunt at their farm. They killed thirty stags, two jackals and a leopard, and afterwards sat in front of a blazing fire and drank and talked. Denys stayed for dinner, then – since it was late – for the night. The next morning Keren drove him into Nairobi, where they lunched together. By this time she was madly in love – she wrote to her sister: 'It is seldom one meets someone one is immediately in sympathy with and gets along so well with, and what a marvellous thing talent and intelligence is . . . I think it is extremely rare to meet one's ideal personified.' Then Denys left for Egypt. They were not to be together again until the following year, at the end of the war. Then, when Denys returned sick with fever, and came to the farm, Karen nursed him. We know no details about how and when they became lovers. But there was very little to prevent them. For years, Blix had had affairs – and one-night stands – quite openly. (One night in the Muthaiga Club, he had seen an attractive American girl on safari with her father, and said as an aside: 'She's mine for tonight', as he ambled forward to introduce himself; the next day he announced in the bar that he had been successful.) Blix and Karen remained on warm and friendly terms, but had never been in love, and were even less so now. What is clear is that for Karen, this was a magical time. She was an imaginative person – she had been writing fragments of plays and stories since childhood – but marriage and the hardships of Africa had almost stifled her imagination. Now it was like a rain-starved garden when a storm breaks. In fact, the rains had just begun when Denys was their guest at the farm, and everything grew green, and the coffee blossomed. Karen wrote lyrically to her sister: 'it is beautiful here, a paradise on earth.' Shortly afterwards Denys took her out alone on safari around Mount Kenya. There are no letters to describe their time together, but she was the only woman he ever took with him alone on safari.

After this blissful time Karen was brought abruptly back to the unpalatable reality of her domestic situation. In her absence Blix had continued to live his careless, hospitable and dissolute life, and now spent little time at the farm, having much to occupy him elsewhere. Financially, the farm was not proving a success – it was lack of rain that would eventually prove their downfall – and Blix tried to supplement their income by poaching ivory. His absences from the farm did nothing to improve things.

Denys had a cottage in the grounds of the Muthaiga Club, and spent much time travelling about the country on business or on safari. He was not to become a professional safari hunter until several years later, and his income came mainly from trading with the Massai. Both men stayed at the farm occasionally, but usually not at the same time. Blix was hardly in a position to complain about Denys's role in Karen's life; but in any case, he liked Denys, and had been known to introduce him as 'my friend, and my wife's lover'. This kind of thing must have made Denys wince, for he was the soul of discretion – not simply because he was an English gentleman, but because he was an intensely private person who hated to be labelled. He stayed for a few days at a time on the farm, but 'he came and left when he wanted to'.

It was, in a sense, a comedy of mutual misunderstanding. Denys certainly loved her in his own way, but had no desire to be a kind of husband. He wanted to come and go as he pleased. Karen, whether she liked it or not, was intensely possessive; she needed and wanted a lover who was also a husband. So their needs remained incompatible.

When at last Karen and Blix decided to part, Blix went to live in Nairobi; she thought she would now be living alone. But not long after, Denys moved his things to the farm, and stayed there between trading expeditions and safaris, generally for a week or two between absences of many months. She wrote: 'When the Gods want to punish us, they give us what we want.' These brief and intense sessions with her lover kept Karen in a state of poised and eager expectation. She described how, when he 'returned from one of his long expeditions, he was starved for talk and found me starved for talk so that we sat over our dinner table into the small hours of the morning, talking of all the things we could think of, and mastering them all and laughing at them'.

Both were good listeners. But he was also a natural teacher, and Karen had been starved of learning since she was a teenager. 'Denys taught me Latin, and to read the Bible and the Greek poets.' He was erudite and well read but never pedantic. In Karen, he found an intelligence to match his own, but in addition, a naturally fertile imagination. In the evenings he would stretch out before the fire and she would tell him long, incredible stories, like Sheherazade in the *Arabian Nights*. 'He would listen, clear eyed, to a long tale, from when it began until it ended. He kept better account of it than I did myself, and at the dramatic appearance of one of the characters would stop me and say "that man died at the beginning of the story, but never mind".'

They also rode, picnicked and camped together, and walked along the game tracks of the Ngong hills in the full moon. At such times, Karen records, she woke in the morning to think 'here I am where I ought to be'. One early morning, out in the hills they came upon a herd of buffalo that seemed to materialize before their eyes; they counted 129 through the morning vapour. With Denys she learned the 'art of moving gently without suddenness, which is the first to be studied by the hunter, more so by hunters with a camera'. They rode often, usually up to the first ridge of the Ngong hills, which they had decided would be a good place to be buried one day. At night they would sit looking up at the sky, which is peculiarly clear in Africa. They believed it was possible to share a star, and that watching the same star, the distance between them would vanish.

True Love Stories

His contributions to the household were the luxuries of life: wines, books, pictures, records and cigars. (He loved music, and gave her many records – Stravinsky was a particular favourite.) He was a perfectionist in all things; this was not confined merely to choosing the best possible equipment whatever he was doing. So when he was to return, Karen polished the silver and filled the house with flowers. And when he was there, she wore simple but elegant cotton dresses or a riding habit, always with wide-brimmed hats; but at night she and Denys would dress for dinner. She took pleasure in beautiful clothes, and when things were going well, ordered them from a Paris couturier. She could look very beautiful, and used belladonna in her eyes, which gave them a luminous sparkle, so they looked enormous. When Denys returned from safaris he brought her special gifts, sometimes leopard or cheetah pelts, 'which could be fashioned into coats or hats in Paris'. On one visit to Abyssinia he found a ring of soft gold which he gave her. She wore it on her wedding finger until three months before his final flight to Mombasa, when he transferred it to his own hand.

Yet much as she adored and needed Denys, she found it hard to accept that he was never with her for long. When he was away she rarely heard from him, and was never sure when he would return. This was not selfishness on his part, but due to the practical difficulty of communication across hundreds of miles of open country with no postal facilities. He did what he could to alleviate her misery, and occasionally she would wake to find a Massai warrior standing outside her house, bringing the message that Denys would be back soon.

At the approach of his Hudson car, she would experience a great surge of joy. Sometimes when she was out in the coffee field 'he would set the gramophone going, and as I came riding back at sunset, the melody streaming towards

136

Karen Blixen, author of *Out of Africa*

me in the clear cool air of the evening would announce his presence to me, as if he had been laughing at me, which he often did'. The uncertainty, the element of surprise, intensified delight in each return, adding a poignancy which, if she had known when to expect him, would have lost some of its excitement.

As soon as Denys arrived all her problems vanished. She wrote to her brother at such a time: 'I am, as you know, one of the happiest people on earth. Despite everything, I think life is wonderful, wonderful, and that the earth is a marvellous place to be in.' But he imposed terms which were hard for her to accept; he insisted that neither would try to possess the other, they would live parallel, but separate lives. When he was with her she did feel no regret about these limitations; the days were rapturous, despite the almost demoniacal possessiveness she experienced when she knew he was about to leave again.

During his absences he tried to alleviate the depression he knew she felt by arranging for friends to visit to help break the monotony. She enjoyed the cheerful social life of the colony; but her servant Kamante sometimes saw her put her head down on her arms and cry helplessly. She wrote: 'At times, life on the farm was very lonely and in the still-ness of the evenings, when the minutes dripped from the clock, life seemed to be dripping out of you with them.'

In spite of which, she had too much character to indulge in self-pity. Publicly she maintained that she cared nothing for convention, and generally this was true; but secretly she longed for the security and the open acknowledgement of love that marriage to Denys would provide. But she knew this was impossible. He would feel that he was a captive. When he arrived she always knew he would soon be off again, but at least 'he brought with him the enormous sky, the plains and the forest'.

In 1925 the divorce from Blix was finalized. Karen was

now alone running the coffee farm. This suited her well; she loved the land and the people who depended upon her. But the basic problems remained: that the farm was a little too high up for coffee, and rainfall was inadequate. Blix advised her to grow blue gum trees for firewood instead, but she would not hear of it. She was determined to succeed with coffee. In the meantime the shareholders, her family in Denmark were becoming anxious. They had been delighted to see the back of Blix for financial as well as moral reasons; but the farm was still running at a loss. They suggested she should sell. To her it was unthinkable, she felt that her life had begun with the farm and she could not let it go. So for the moment Denys and her mother lent her money to carry on.

That year Denys took up hunting professionally. He already had a great reputation for his skill; now he was less interested in shooting game than in photographic safaris – for he was increasingly aware of the need for conservation as the great herds dwindled, set upon by hunters shooting indiscriminately from vehicles. If he had lived, it seems likely he would have been at the forefront of the conservation movement which began a few years later. Now, he left Karen for five months while he took out an American millionaire named Patterson, who was interested in photography, and who had made 'a hideous amount of money' inventing a patent cash register.

In 1929 when Edward, the Prince of Wales, was in East Africa, Denys, as the foremost white hunter, was chosen to take him on safari. The Prince's visit had the whole colony in a state of immense excitement; lavish social functions were arranged, the state rooms at Government House were redecorated, and colonial wives perfected their royal curtsies. Karen was largely excluded from the social events of the royal visit because, as a divorcee, she could not be formally presented to the Prince. Worse, in August, Blix had married again, so now to her outrage, there were two Baroness Blixens.

In fact, the Prince himself sought her out, informally inviting himself to the farm to watch one of the impressive traditional African dances. Before she came to Africa, Karen had learned to cook from a Parisian chef, because she thought 'it would be amusing to eat well in Africa' and she had passed on her knowledge to her African cook Kamante, who now excelled himself, producing an exquisite meal of lobster.

The Prince and his brother were keen sportsmen and with Denys's guidance, shot some excellent specimens of the major game animals. (Before they departed from Nairobi, their spirit of conquest was also exercised on a number of attractive wives.) Denys took the royal party to Tanzania in search of lions, but warned that they might be unsuccessful: 'Africa does not wear her heart on her sleeve, even for a Prince.' But Blix (who knew Tanzania well) was called to the rescue, and in a short while the Prince was being photographed with his foot on a dead lion.

It was at this point that the safari was brought to an abrupt halt by the news that the King was seriously ill; to his annoyance, Prince Edward had to leave at once. Denys was invited to sail back to England with the royal party, but declined in order to be with Karen for Christmas.

But things at Ngong were not going well. The farm was still losing money, and the shareholders pressed Karen to sell. Denys's safaris meant that he was spending longer and longer periods away. Permanently worried about the future, Karen found it impossible to conceal her growing possessiveness from Denys. When she heard that the second Baroness Blixen had been on safari with the Prince she felt, irrationally, that she had been betrayed. So from the moment he came home, the thought of his departure tormented her – her first question to him was 'How long?'

When he was with her the time sped by, but there were times when she could not refrain from mentioning her discontent. Denys was forced to become increasingly reticent about departure dates, or plans for future safaris. Karen was aware that this kind of discord is often present in the household of hunters, and that many marriages fail to survive it, but her insecurity was increased by the fact that she was not even married.

In her determination to keep the place she loved, and to protect the Africans who lived there, she insisted that she could make the farm profitable. If it had been turned over to mixed crops and cattle ranching – for which it was highly suitable – it could have been a viable concern. But to do this she would need all of the land, and this would mean throwing 'her' people out, and she was not willing even to consider it. Even Denys advised her that she must try something else. He lent her money to continue, but refused to become further involved. Things had now reached a point where everything depended upon whether the coffee crop in 1929 was good.

That year Denys took up flying again and went to England to requalify to pilot his own plane. Karen was also away most of the year in Denmark – her mother was ill. She received news of the farm by post, and learned that in May there had been a frost which had damaged the berries. In October she briefly joined Denys in England and met his family, who although polite, were not enthusiastic about her. Denys's brother Lord Winchilsea wrote in his diary 'she is trying to take possession of Denys. It won't do.'

When she arrived back at Mombasa – sixteen years after her first arrival – it was Farah, her Somali servant, who rowed out to meet her. At first she avoided asking the question she had been thinking about continuously during the journey. When she finally brought herself to speak, Farah told her the crop this year had only been forty tons.

True Love Stories

They needed at least sixty to survive. She realized that her days of farming were numbered.

When Denys returned to Nairobi, he brought with him a bright yellow two-seater De Haviland Gypsy Moth aeroplane. A runway was built for it at the farm, and he took Karen flying. Her descriptions of her flights are euphoric. This new-found liberty brought a new intensity to their relationship. High up over the Ngong hills she could look down on her farm. 'The loveliest days . . . a magical effect . . . I think it is doubtful whether greater happiness could exist for me than flying over Ngong with him.' Looking down from more than 1,000 feet, she found that even disasters have a certain beauty of pattern, and began to come to terms with her destiny.

When Denys vanished on safari with an American millionaire and his wife, Karen suddenly felt she must make one last attempt to save the farm. She wrote asking him for financial help; back from the bush by runner came his unconditional refusal.

The auction took place a month later in December. The buyer, a Nairobi businessman called Remy Martin, planned to turn the farm into a suburb of expensive homes; the district would be called 'Karen' in her honour. He chivalrously informed her that she could occupy the house while building went on. 'I would', she replied with a sad smile, 'prefer to live in the middle of the Sahara desert, than in the suburb of "Karen".'

Now there was no longer a farm to return to, it was clear that Denys's detachment was complete. He loved her, but may well have been relieved that fate had intervened to break the pattern. When he was not on safari or attending to his businesses, he still took her flying, and when they spoke about her leaving for Denmark it was obvious that he was genuinely grieved. But he was quite determined not to break the rule they had both accepted at an early stage in their relationship: 'I will never come for pity. I will come for pleasure.'

In *Out of Africa*, written seven years later, Karen mentions that Denys was now staying with a bachelor friend in Nairobi, because he could not bear to see the house full of packing cases and empty rooms. But in fact friends were aware that there had been a rift between them, over another woman.

This, it later emerged, was Beryl Markham, who would become the first person to fly the Atlantic east to west. Beryl had adored Denys for years, but had proved no rival to Karen Blixen. Beryl was then living in the cottage on the grounds of the Muthaiga Club and it was here that Denys spent much of the first two months of his last year.

One night when Denys came out to the farm to dine, he took back the Abyssinian ring of soft gold and put it on his own hand, because, according to Karen, '. . . he thought I might . . . give it away. It was a few days before he went to Mombasa and in this way the ring was buried with him.'

Denys was preparing to go on a photographic safari with Patterson, but first he had some business in Mombasa. Karen wanted to fly down with him, but he refused, saying that he wanted to look over Tsavo game reserve for elephant on the return journey, and that he would be spending a night in the bush; this meant that he would need to take a servant, so there would be no room for Karen. She was miserable to see him go. She wrote subsequently: 'he was subject to a special kind of moods and forebodings . . . The last days before he started on his journey to the coast, he was . . . absent-minded, as if sunk in contemplation, but when I spoke of it he laughed at me.' A friend later said of him, 'He did not fear death . . . he feared old age and dependency.' On 10 May 1931, Denys left for Mombasa with his reluctant Kikuyu servant

Kamau, who hated flying. As he landed, he somehow chipped the wooden propeller on a coral fragment. Immediately he wired Nairobi for a replacement and his friend Tom sent down a mechanic with a spare. By 13 May the refitting was complete and Denys and Kamau headed off for Tsavo. After an hour of scouting for elephant, Kamau became airsick, so they landed near the house of Denys's friend, the district commissioner, and stayed there the night.

Next morning, the family came out to the airstrip to see them off, and Denys asked the DC's wife if she would like to go for a spin. She accepted, but her younger daughter, who normally had no fear of planes, unaccountably grabbed her and implored her not to go, howling and protesting so loudly that her mother finally changed her mind. 'Another time,' said Denys briefly, clambering into the cockpit.

Kamau got into the front seat. Moments later, the yellow flying machine taxied off and then soared into the air. They watched it circle overhead, then turn in the direction of Nairobi. A few moments later, they heard the engine splutter and the plane plummeted down, out of their range of vision. Stunned and appalled they watched helplessly as clouds of black smoke billowed into the air. Denys's friend Hunter was at the scene in time to see the plane burst into flames. It was impossible to get near, the heat was intense. News of the crash reached Nairobi before it reached Ngong. Karen had expected to see Denys for lunch at Lady Macmillan's house; but first she had some shopping to do in Nairobi. She records feeling that everyone she met seemed to turn away from her, barely returning her greetings: 'I began to feel as lonely in Nairobi as on a desert island.' Lady Macmillan broke the news. Karen, later wrote, '. . . at the sound of Denys's name . . . I knew and understood everything.'

After Karen left Africa, her friend Gustav Mohr
wrote to her of a strange thing that happened by
Denys's grave:
'The Masai have reported to the District
Commissioner at Ngong, that many times, at
sunrise and sunset, they have seen lions on Finch
Hatton's grave in the Hills. A lion and a lioness
have come there, and stood, or lain, on the
grave for a long time . . . I suppose that the level
place makes a good site for the lions, from there
they can have a view over the plain, and the
cattle and game on it.'

Denys was buried high up in the Ngong hills, in the
place they had chosen for their graves. It had a wide view
of the grasslands and in the distance, the farm. Later his
brother marked the spot with a stone inscribed: 'He
prayeth well, who loveth well / Both man and bird and
beast', from one of Denys's favourite poems, 'The Ancient
Mariner'.

Karen was treated by everyone as Denys's widow.
Friends did not even try to console her, only to give her
love and sympathy. She placed a strip of white cotton
between two poles over the grave and in the last few
weeks she remained on the farm, she would climb up
onto the roof so that she could see the place Denys was
buried.

Not long after Denys's death, Karen Blixen left Africa for
ever; some years later, now living in her birthplace,
Denmark, she began to write the book which begins: 'I had
a farm in Africa at the foot of the Ngong hills.'

Out of Africa would become a classic and a best-seller, but it was for her volumes of strange gothic tales, written under the pseudonym Isak Dinesen, that she eventually became famous. When *Seven Gothic Tales* appeared in 1934, with their old-fashioned style and nineteenth-century settings – ghosts, duels, floods – they achieved immediate popularity, for many readers were tired of the brutal realism of Joyce and Hemingway and Dos Passos. The stories have been described as 'exotic, self-parodying melodramas', and one critic commented that Isak Dinesen 'wandered in rather like a reveller strayed from a masked ball who had forgotten to take off his fancy dress'. Many of these were the stories invented by Karen as she and Denys spent long evenings together by the fire at her farm.

Out of Africa, published in 1937, was praised for its sensitive evocation of Kenya. Yet to anyone who knows her life story, it seems odd that she hardly ever mentions her lover directly. She writes a great deal about the Africans and the white settlers who were her friends, but she says very little about Denys, whose existence had been central to her, and who had made her years in Africa the most important of her life. Only after her death, when her letters and journals became available, did the complete picture of those years become clear.

During the Second World War, Denmark was occupied by the Germans, and her second volume of stories, *Winter Tales*, appeared in 1942. Also during this period she wrote a novel in Danish, *The Angelic Avenger* (1944, under the pseudonym Pierre Andrezel), which was an attack on the Germans, but so subtle that they failed to recognize it as a piece of anti-Nazi propaganda.

Later publications – *Last Tales* (1957), *Anecdotes of Destiny* (1958) and *Shadows on the Grass* (1961 – another volume about those years in Africa) added to her reputation, and since her death in 1962, at the age of seventy-seven, she has been accepted as a great European classic.

Karen Blixen

Yet it is possible that, but for her love affair with Denys Finch Hatton, Karen Blixen might never have allowed her creative imagination to take flight and her name would now be unknown to us.

Chapter Ten

Scarlett and Rhett

On an April morning in 1935, Harold Latham, vice-president of the Macmillan publishing company, arrived in Atlanta, Georgia, looking for new writers. During the 1920s, America had turned into a nation of readers, with the result that authors found themselves in a buyer's market. There were more publishers than new books to go around. This is why Harold Latham had decided to go south, looking for unpublished writers.

The trip had so far not been a success. The manuscripts he had been offered were unreadable. Once in his hotel room, Latham rang up Macmillan's Atlanta office, and was disappointed when they told him they had nothing much to show him.

Latham tried ringing the New York office, to speak to Lois Dwight Cole, who had once been their Atlanta representative. Did she happen to know any writers in Atlanta?

'Well there's Peggy Mitchell Marsh,' Lois said reluctantly, 'I know she's been working on a novel about the Civil War for a long time, but for some reason, she's not willing to show it to anybody.'

'Who is she?' Latham asked.

'Ten years ago she worked on the *Atlanta Journal Magazine*, and got herself quite a reputation. Now she's married, and as far as I know, her husband is the only one who has seen the manuscript.'

Latham wanted to know how to contact Peggy Marsh. The best way, said Lois, was to telephone another contributor to the *Atlanta Journal Magazine*, Medora Field Perkerson – she was married to the magazine's editor-in-chief, Angus Perkerson.

By a pleasant coincidence, Latham was going to lunch with the Perkersons the following day. He rang Medora Perkerson at her office, and asked whether she could persuade Peggy Marsh to join them for lunch.

'I'll try,' said Medora, 'but I may not be successful. She doesn't get around a great deal these days.'

In fact, Medora found the perfect excuse. Her husband had been called away, and she asked Peggy Marsh if she would be willing to come along and act as co-hostess of the lunch party.

When Latham – who was bespectacled, pot-bellied and unmarried – met Peggy Marsh, he thought there must be some mistake. She only looked about twenty. She was pretty, pert, and less than five feet tall. She wore her hair in the style of a flapper of the 1920s. But at lunch, she talked brilliantly and charmingly, with a sense of humour, and a taste for mildly indecent anecdotes that surprised him.

Towards the end of the lunch, Latham said that he heard she had written a novel. Avoiding his eyes, Peggy Marsh said: 'I have no novel.'

Outside in the car, he raised the subject again. This time, she confessed that she was writing a novel, 'but it's too early to talk about it.' It was about the South she said but she was sure that it would not sell, because 'it's about a woman who is in love with another woman's husband, and they do nothing about it, and because there are only four Goddamns and one dirty word in it'. When he said he would still like to see the manuscript, she said that if she ever completed it, she would make sure that he was the first to see it.

The next day, Peggy Marsh collected a group of hopeful young writers, and took them along to tea with Latham.

Once again, he raised the subject of the manuscript, and once again, she insisted that she had nothing to show him.

Now, driving one of the young hopefuls home, she confessed that the reason she would not show the manuscript to Macmillan was because 'it's so lousy I'm ashamed of it'.

To her fury, the girl replied: 'I wouldn't take you for the type who could write a successful novel.' When Peggy indignantly asked her what she meant, she replied: 'You lack the seriousness necessary to be a novelist.'

Peggy dropped off the young hopeful, rushed home, and pulled out dozens of tattered manila envelopes stuffed with typescript. They were stashed in odd places all over the house, including under the bath. She looked at the first chapter – or rather, at the envelope that contained a dozen or so versions of the first chapter – and decided that it needed to be rewritten immediately. Latham was leaving Atlanta in a few hours' time, but she settled down at her typewriter, and pounded away. Finally, she rushed to the hotel, telephoned Latham's room, and told him she had brought him her manuscript.

When he came down, and saw the two giant piles of manila envelopes – each more than three feet tall – he was slightly shaken. He had to buy a cheap cardboard suitcase to pack it in. And when he got onto the train and opened the first envelope, he saw one of the most dog-eared typescripts he had ever seen in his life. Sometimes, the pages were unreadable because of all the crossings-out and substitutions. Latham was tempted to put it in its envelope, take it back to New York unread, and send it back to her with a note saying he would like to see it when she had it in some kind of order.

But since he had nothing else to do, and since he was still curious, he began to read.

Several hours later, he was still reading. Peggy Marsh

Margaret Mitchell, author of *Gone with the Wind*

had given him the manuscript of the novel that would be called *Gone with the Wind*.

A few weeks later, Peggy Marsh had a car accident – her second in a year. Swerving to avoid another car, she ran on to the kerb, and was thrown against the steering wheel. Two weeks after this, an enthusiastic guest waving a bottle of whisky in the air managed to hit her on the head with it, knocking her unconscious.

Recuperating from these misfortunes, she decided that she would like to begin work once more on her novel. She wrote to Latham asking him to return it. In reply, he wrote:

'Please hold off your request. I am very enthusiastic about the possibilities your book presents. I believe if it finished properly it will have every chance of a very considerable success.'

A few days later, she received a telegram from Lois Cole that read: 'MACMILLAN TERRIBLE EXCITED YOUR BOOK I AM MOST EXCITED OF ALL.' Latham followed this up with a telegram saying that his advisers shared his enthusiasm for her novel, and they would like to make an immediate contract with a $500 advance, half on signing and the rest on the delivery of the completed manuscript.

Peggy was not sure whether she wanted a contract. But when her husband came home from work, he telegraphed Latham accepting.

The first reader to submit a report was also enthusiastic. He had only one minor criticism – the ending of the book struck him as disappointing, with Rhett Butler walking out on the heroine. At this stage, the heroine's first name was Pansy, and Harold Latham objected to this, suggesting that the word had 'unpleasant connotations'.

The task of editing, rewriting, and bridging the gaps in the typescript, was so exhausting that, in January 1936, she had to spend two weeks in bed.

Scarlett and Rhett

In February, Macmillan announced its spring list, and placed *Gone with the Wind* close to the top. Enquiries from Hollywood immediately began to pour in. But when the film moguls saw the vast proof, they lost their enthusiasm. Irving Thalberg told Louis B. Mayer at MGM: 'Forget it, Louis. No Civil War picture ever made a nickle.' He was right – there had been several, and they had all been flops.

Peggy acquired herself a female agent, Annie Laurie Williams, who turned down an offer of $40,000 from Jack Warner, of Warner Brothers insisting she would not take less than $65,000.

On 15 April 1936, the Book-of-the-Month Club chose *Gone with the Wind* as their main selection, and agreed to take 50,000 copies to begin with.

Later that month, *Publishers Weekly* brought out an advance review that described *Gone with the Wind* as 'very possibly the greatest American novel'.

By May, it was so clear the book was going to be a success that Latham ordered a further $5,000 to be paid to her. Copies of the book sent to various Southern newspapers aroused enthusiasm, and suddenly, everybody in Atlanta wanted to throw parties for her. She accepted all the invitations, but still flatly refused to go to New York for the publication.

On publication day, 30 June 1936, Edwin Granberry in the *New York Sun,* compared Margaret Mitchell with Tolstoy, Hardy and Dickens. In the *New York Post,* Herschel Brickell referred to it as a book that would 'pass into the permanent body of American literature'. Already, there were 100,000 copies in print. Within three weeks of publication, it had sold 178,000. In the next six months it sold a million copies, 50,000 of them in one day. Over the next few years, it would sell almost three million copies in America, and a million in England. It was also translated into twenty-

153

two languages. *Gone with the Wind* became the greatest publishing sensation of all time.

Peggy Marsh was never to write another novel, or even as much as a short story. She had put all of her life, all of herself into the book. And there was a sense in which, with the publication of the book, her life was over.

Margaret Munnerlyn Mitchell was born on 5 November 1900, in Atlanta, Georgia. Her mother's forebears were French Huguenots. Her father's ancestors were Scots. Eugene Mitchell was a lawyer, specializing in real estate and patents. He was a mild, easygoing character, whose greatest passion was the history of the American South. His wife Maybelle was a small, determined woman who was an ardent suffragette, who frequently held political meetings in her front room. She bore two children: Stephens, born in 1895, and Margaret (later Peggy), five years his junior. Margaret inherited her mother's determination, and some of her tendency to egoism. Her biographer Anne Edwards comments: 'Like Scarlett O'Hara, Peggy Mitchell was never able to endure a conversation of which she was not the subject.'

Peggy grew up a tomboy. She admired her brother, and liked to join in games with his friends – like having battles with mud balls. (Too small to throw them, Margaret had to be contented with supplying them to the front-line troops.)

Margaret was also accident-prone, and to some extent, this helps to explain how and why she became a writer. She absorbed from her father his love of history, and during her long spells in bed, recovering from accidents, she studied a lot of it. The first major accident took place when she was three years old, when her skirts began to burn as she stood in front of an open fire that suddenly flared. The burns to her legs took weeks to heal. When she was ten, she tried to turn a galloping horse too quickly, and was crushed underneath it. Her left leg was badly damaged and for a long time she walked with a limp. She continued to be accident-prone for the rest of her life, and as often as not, it was the left leg that was injured again. It was during some of these later periods of recuperation that she worked on *Gone with the Wind*.

Atlanta was not an old city. It had been founded in the mid-1840s, and was burned in September 1864 by General Sherman's troops, after which Sherman ravaged the country between Atlanta and the sea. The Civil War would come to an end in the following April.

Margaret learned much of her Civil War history from her father, and the rest from veterans on whose knees she sat throughout long afternoons when the veterans reminisced about Robert E. Lee.

At the age of five, after her first day at school, she told her mother that she hated arithmetic and did not want to go back. Her mother's response was to spank her with a hair brush, then drive her in the carriage past the long series of run-down stately homes, which had once been the residences of rich plantation owners. Maybelle Mitchell concluded with a sermon on the general instability and insecurity of the world, and how education was the only way of arming yourself against it. The next day, Margaret returned to school. She was a non-stop talker, and by the time she was nine, was already producing some surprisingly mature prose. Her abilities as a storyteller are attested by the fact that even her elder brother – five years her senior – listened fascinated to her tales of adventure and ghost stories. On one occasion, she adapted a Civil War novel called *The Traitor* and staged it in her sitting room. Inevitably, she herself played the lead (even though it was supposed to be played by a male). To her surprise, her father reacted by giving her a spanking on the grounds that she had infringed the author's copyright.

Unfortunately, she was always curiously humble about

her literary work. In the back cover of her first (unfinished) novel, she wrote that born writers knew how to make their characters into living people; while 'made' writers merely create dummies – and added, 'that's how I know I'm a "made" writer.'

By the age of sixteen, she was turning into a pretty teenager. She still talked too much, and enjoyed giving orders – one classmate commented: 'Margaret was only happy if she could boss people around' – but young men began to look at her with interest. When America entered the Great War in April 1917, her brother Stephens joined up. Margaret learned to drive, and made it her business to drive to army camps and bring back young officers for the weekend. She was a natural flirt, but drew the line at kissing. Although she was a rebel, her rebelliousness never extended to sexual matters.

In 1918, she met a young lieutenant named Clifford Henry, who came from New York. Like her father, he was something of a dreamer, and enjoyed reciting poetry. The two of them were soon convinced they were in love, and on the night before he was due to sail for Europe, they became secretly engaged on the Mitchells' veranda.

So far, Margaret had been educated at the nearby Washington Seminary – her mother was a devout Catholic – but now she decided that she wanted to continue her education in the North. She was sent to Smith College in Massachusetts. At this point, she had decided that she wanted to become a doctor. At first, she found it disconcertingly impersonal after the South, and among these sophisticated young ladies – many of whom had spent a great deal of time in Europe and spoke fluent French – she felt herself drab, dowdy and inexperienced. But her warm and amusing personality soon made her a number of close friends. She had only been there a few weeks when she heard that Clifford Henry had been killed in battle. Anne

Edwards, who researched into Henry's background, was later to discover that he had strong homosexual tendencies.

Her brother Stephens returned safely from the war. But a few weeks later, in January 1919, Maybelle Mitchell died of pneumonia. Margaret was on her way home, summoned by telegram, at the time, but arrived too late. After a few more months at Smith College, she decided to return to Atlanta, to look after her father and brother.

She proved to be an efficient housekeeper. But it did not take her long to realize that, unless something happened to rescue her, the role of dutiful daughter would continue until she became an old maid. As usual when she was plunged in self-doubt, her unconscious mind seems to have taken a hand – she tried to make her horse jump a stone wall and landed with the horse on top of her. Again, it was the left leg that took most of the damage. She was in bed for months, and when she got up, had to wear low-heeled shoes.

In August 1920, Margaret – now preferring to be known as Peggy – went to a costume ball dressed as a little girl of the pre-Civil War period. Her escort was one of the doctors she had met as a result of her accident. That night, she saw for the first time a tall young man – who towered fifteen inches above her – named Berrien Kinnard Upshaw, who was known to everyone as Red. He was a University of Georgia football player, and had a cleft chin, red hair and green eyes. He also had a high, square forehead, high cheekbones and a long chin – a combination that makes his photographs resemble Frankenstein's monster as played by Boris Karloff. But none of the women in the room seemed to have the least doubt that he was the handsomest man there.

The two were instantly attracted. For the rest of the evening, the ringleted southern belle with her poke bonnet danced with the tall pirate whose head was so far above her that his chin did not even touch her hair. She later learned that the pirate costume was appropriate – Red Upshaw kept himself solvent by smuggling bootleg liquor.

Peggy's friends found Upshaw coarse, and some of them reported that he drank too much and had a reputation for womanizing. None of this bothered Peggy. She herself enjoyed telling improper anecdotes, and scandalized the elderly ladies of Atlanta by smoking and drinking.

That autumn, Red Upshaw decided to leave college – where his grades were poor – and become a full-time bootlegger. Peggy thought he was risking his future, and the two of them quarrelled. The break was made easier by the fact that she was now mixing with her peers in the Atlanta social set, and had officially become a 'debutante'. In fact, she found most of her new friends rather stuffy, but in a small town like Atlanta, there was not much choice.

At a party at the Junior League, her attempt to remedy the stiffness backfired. Peggy had always loved dressing up in costume. With a tall, good-looking student from Georgia Tech, she decided to perform an Apache dance, in a slitted black skirt with black stockings. They made it realistic and highly suggestive, with Peggy occasionally bending so far back in her partner's arms that her head touched the floor. In Paris or New York it would not have raised an eyebrow; in Atlanta, it scandalized the matrons sitting around the walls. The result was that Peggy failed to receive the invitation she expected to become a member of the Junior League. She felt angry, humiliated and helpless. She was the kind of person who took setbacks to heart, and brooded on them for a long time.

It was nearly two years before she met Red Upshaw again – at the club of which they both became members. Peggy was now wearing short skirts and bobbed hair, and flirtatiousness was becoming part of her personality. With her wit and her abilities as a conversationalist, she was always the centre of attention in the Peachtree Yachting

Club. She and Upshaw were natural companions. He was obviously intrigued by the fact that she could display such natural sexuality, and yet remain so determinedly chaste. He introduced her to a young man with whom he was sharing an apartment, John Marsh, who was quiet, serious and bespectacled. Peggy's father liked Marsh as much as he disliked Upshaw. And Marsh was soon as determined to win Peggy as Upshaw was – the difference being that Marsh's intentions were honourable.

Peggy obviously found it delightful to have two men in love with her, and – inevitably – played them off against one another. Marsh had been an English teacher, but was now in the magazine business as a copy editor. When the two men began to find it tiresome to court Peggy in the presence of the other, they started tossing a coin to decide which of them should spend the first half of the evening with her, and which should have her for the more interesting hours.

Peggy herself was experiencing a problem. She responded intensely to Upshaw's sexuality, and there were times when she had to remind herself of her strict Catholic upbringing and her mother's admonitions to prevent herself from yielding. Upshaw finally gave in. If possessing her meant marrying her, then he was willing to take that alarming step.

Peggy Mitchell and Red Upshaw were married on 2 September 1922. With typical gallantry and self-effacement, John Marsh had agreed to be their best man.

Immediately after the wedding reception, they climbed into Red's bright green automobile, and drove away to spend the night in his apartment. After that, they went to meet Upshaw's parents in North Carolina.

Peggy Mitchell failed to record precisely why the marriage ended so soon. It is possible that she found Red Upshaw's lovemaking brutal and lacking in finesse. It is possible that, having paid such a high price for her surrender, Upshaw quickly became bored. He was fundamentally an adventurer; she was fundamentally a middle-class girl who craved security. She may also have irritated him by telling him how much she had adored Clifford Henry.

Back in Atlanta, they moved into Peggy's home with her father and brother. Her father still disliked Upshaw, but since he was now his daughter's husband, had to make the best of it. So did Peggy. She wanted her husband to find a regular job. He found the idea boring, and could not understand why, if she was in love with him, she was unwilling to leave home and take a chance. She had allowed him to sweep her off her feet, but she had a stubborn, determined, cautious streak, that meant that it was unlikely she would allow it to happen again.

She wrote about her troubles to John Marsh, who was now an editor in Washington. Eventually, at her request, Marsh returned to Atlanta to try to persuade Red Upshaw to drink less. It was too late; by the time he returned to Atlanta in December 1922, Peggy and Upshaw had decided to get divorced. Three months after their marriage, Red Upshaw walked out on her, and drove back to North Carolina.

Now Peggy decided it was time to get herself a job. By exaggerating her experience, she persuaded the *Atlanta Journal* to take her on as a reporter. Her first article – an interview with an Atlanta woman who had been in Rome at the time of Mussolini's takeover – appeared on the last day of 1922.

Within a year, she was one of the *Journal*'s star reporters. She enjoyed meeting people, and had the ability to make them talk freely. She liked the sense of adventure it gave her to drive around the countryside and meet strangers. When a sculptor began to carve faces of Civil War generals on the side of a mountain, she even allowed herself to be photographed suspended from the fifteenth floor of a skyscraper in a window-cleaner's chair, to describe to the reader exactly what it felt like.

The relationship with John Marsh had turned into a warm but non-physical friendship. He read and edited Peggy's articles – it was a job at which he excelled – and seemed to accept the fact that she preferred them to remain 'just friends'.

One day in July 1923, six months after her separation from Red Upshaw, she found him waiting in front of her house. She had told John that she never wanted to see her husband again, but now they were face to face, the old magic operated, and she invited him in.

What happened next has never been exactly determined. She admitted that they spent ten minutes talking in the sitting room, then went upstairs to the bedroom. Upshaw seems to have understood this as an invitation to undress her. When she resisted, he beat her and blacked her eye – later, in the divorce court, she was to deny that he raped her, although this also seems probable. Her screams brought their servant Bessie to the bedroom door, in time to see Red Upshaw striding downstairs, and Peggy running after him and screaming that he should get out of her house. Before he left, he turned and hit her in the eye. The encounter left her so bruised and battered that she had to spend two weeks in hospital.

After beating his wife, Upshaw went to Marsh's apartment, told him what had happened and borrowed some money from him. Then he left. It was not until he saw Peggy in her darkened hospital room that Marsh realized just how badly she had been beaten. He bought her a pistol, and told her to use it if the necessity arose.

The divorce came through in October 1924. Meanwhile, Peggy had continued to work on the *Journal*, and to consolidate her position as a local celebrity. As entertainment editor, she interviewed a number of film stars, including Rudolph Valentino, who lifted her off her feet and carried her into his hotel suite – but only as far as the sitting room.

In December 1924 John Marsh suffered an absurd and undignified illness. He began to hiccup, and continued for week after week. It so exhausted him that he had to be taken into hospital. Drugs and sedatives had no effect – he continued to hiccup in his sleep. After more than a month of this, he was so weak that he seemed on the point of death, and had to be kept in an oxygen tent. It was forty-two days before he was able to control the hiccups for long enough to tell her that he loved her. By this time, the prospect of losing him had convinced her that she loved him too. They were married on 4 July 1925.

Because John had been away from work for so long, and incurred huge medical bills, they were heavily in debt. They moved into a tiny apartment, which they called the 'Dump', hired a part-time cook, and turned the narrow hallway into an office where Peggy could type. It was on this typewriter that Peggy wrote a series of articles about Civil War generals, about which the editor of the *Atlanta Journal* was enthusiastic, and readers even more so. After that, she began a long story with a typical Jazz Age setting – young people at a party who drink too much bootleg liquor, and are then involved in a car chase, in which the hero gets injured. The heroine was called Pansy, and bore obvious resemblances to Peggy. The hero bore such a close resemblance to Red Upshaw that Peggy finally had to break off the story. She found it impossible to write fiction without it turning into autobiography.

Her biographer Anne Edwards notes that, as long as she was working for the *Journal*, she was always in excellent health – in spite of the amount she drank and smoked. But as soon as she retired – midway through 1926 – things began to go wrong. Her husband's doctors had concluded that there was nothing basically wrong with him, and that his illnesses were basically psychosomatic. The same seemed to be true of Peggy. With nothing much to do, her unconscious mind seemed to make up for her boredom by plaguing her with illnesses.

The answer, she decided, was to write. She began a story about an aristocratic Southern family in decline. The heroine was in love with a mulatto who was the son of a slave. After the lover is killed, the heroine is forced by her neighbours to leave her home.

The story ran to 15,000 words, and Peggy was convinced that it was good. Her husband disagreed – he thought that it was full of good things, but that on the whole it was a failure. In a state of depression, Peggy had one of her inevitable accidents – her car skidded in the rain and hit a tree. She escaped with a sprained ankle, but it was so painful that she was confined to her bed. She was forced to read books from the local library – many of them about the Civil War. One day, John came home without any books, but with a stack of writing paper. He explained that she seemed to have read her way through most of the books in the local library. If she wanted to read, he told her, she would have to write a book herself.

The next day – in January 1927 – she sat down at her typewriter and typed the words: 'She had never understood either of the men she loved and so she lost them both.'

It was to be the seed of *Gone with the Wind*.

The next day she wrote the last scene of the novel – the one in which Red Upshaw walks out on Pansy (she had salvaged the name from her Jazz Age story). It was an odd way of working, but she had picked it up on the *Journal*, where she preferred writing the first and then the last paragraphs of an article so she knew exactly where she had to go in between. That evening, John read the scene, and made various suggestions and corrections. The next day she retyped it, incorporating his corrections, then returned to the beginning of the book.

It flowed easily. She turned out to be a natural writer of fiction. Sometimes, she was unsure about the ending of a chapter, and would write several endings. Sometimes, uncertain of some historical detail, she would push the unfinished chapter into one of her manila envelopes and go on to the next. As she continued to write 2,000 words a day, the pile of envelopes increased, until there was hardly room for them in the tiny apartment.

Inevitably, the novel was autobiographical, inevitably, Pansy O'Hara was Margaret Mitchell as she saw herself, attractive, headstrong and self-willed. The daughter of a wealthy plantation owner, she falls in love with the poetic and dreamy Ashley Dukes, heir to the plantation next door. Ashley is obviously an idealized version of Clifford Henry. In the opening scene of the novel, Pansy discovers to her horror that Ashley has proposed to another girl, his cousin Melanie. Her reaction is to marry Melanie's brother Charles. A year later, Charles is killed in the Civil War, leaving Pansy pregnant. She goes to live in Atlanta with her in-laws, but when Atlanta is burned by Sherman's troups, succeeds in making her way back to her father's plantation, Tara (named after the legendary home of Irish heroes). The countryside is devastated, and when she gets back, she discovers that her father has lost his mind from shock. Her mother is dead. Now the Yankees have left, the only persons left in Tara are her two sisters, Melanie, and a few servants who have stayed behind when the others fled.

Scarlett determines to save Tara at all costs. In the struggle, her character becomes hardened and ruthless, she has to learn to live by the law of the jungle. When she has to pay a tax

Clark Gable and Vivien Leigh in *Gone with the Wind*

demand for $300, she unhesitatingly decides to save Tara by marrying a local store owner, Frank Kennedy, who is engaged to her sister Suellen. Then she borrows money from Rhett Butler, and uses it to buy a sawmill, of which she makes a success, and at last achieves financial security.

Her husband is killed by Yankees, and she marries Rhett, who has made a fortune as a blockade runner during the war. Yet still, Scarlett remains in love with Ashley Dukes. Even the birth of a child fails to reconcile her to her situation. When Rhett realizes that Scarlett has married him for his money, and that she still loves Ashley Dukes, his love for her vanishes. It is only when he is about to walk out on her that she realizes that Rhett was the man she loved all along, and as he walks out with the famous line: 'My dear, I don't give a damn', she vows to get him back again.

Strangely enough, the immense success of *Gone with the Wind* failed to make her happy. It was typical that, on their eleventh wedding anniversary, Peggy's and John's lives were so chaotic that they did not even have time to exchange presents. She wrote to her publisher: 'Life has been so much like a nightmare recently that it was all I could do to stay on my feet.' Peggy Mitchell was basically a small-town girl, whose ambition was to live quietly and peacefully, see a few friends, and spend her days writing and reading about the Civil War. Now the book was published, all this was gone. There was nothing more to write – only endless letters in reply to the sacks full of correspondence that arrived every day.

One morning soon after publication, she received a shock when she answered the telephone and heard Red Upshaw's voice.

'After reading your book I figure you still love me.'

Peggy asked why.

'Because Rhett Butler is obviously modelled after me.'

She denied it and asked him what he wanted. He promised to come and see her some day and tell her in person. Then he hung up.

She was terrified he might sue her for libel, or at least, give some interviews in which he told the story of their marriage. She was neurotically determined to keep it a secret. That morning, she had to sit through a three-hour interview with three Associated Press reporters, and she took care to skip over the period between her mother's death and her marriage to John Marsh.

After the interview, she jumped into her car and drove up into the mountains, from where she wrote eight letters to writers and newspaper reporters explaining how she had run away from the 'hell of fame', and had been forced to run away at a moment's notice with only one small bag. She wrote a letter to the critic Edwin Cranberry, who immediately invited her to come and stay with him. There, in Hickory, North Carolina, she felt she could relax and be anonymous.

The next major event in her life was the announcement that the Hollywood producer David O. Selznick was going to make the film of *Gone with the Wind,* and was looking for a leading man and woman. Clark Gable was chosen fairly quickly to play Rhett Butler, but for the next year, every newspaper in America discussed who would play the part of Scarlett O'Hara. Vivien Leigh was eventually chosen, but that was only the first hurdle. The film ran into endless difficulties with the script, and quickly soared well above its budget. Again and again, it looked as if Selznick had bitten off more than he could chew, and the whole project would collapse. The final triumph of the premiere in Atlanta, on 15 December 1939, was certainly among the most dramatic moments in Hollywood's history.

Her biographer Anne Edwards writes:

'The premiere and the adulation she had received during that week in December had been the apogee of her sudden and meteoric rise to fame. It was not just her fans, but *all* of Atlanta who had paid her homage. It seemed doubtful that anything further could occur in her life that would equal the sense of accomplishment she had felt as she stepped out of the Selznick limousine before the Loew's Grand Theatre, unless it had been the moment when she had stood alone, front and centre of the Grand's stage, waiting for the ovation that was being given her to subside. At that moment, she later confessed to Medora, she felt assured that Atlanta was proud of the film and proud of her, and that she never again need worry about losing the esteem of her hometown folk.'

There was a sense in which the rest of her life was an anticlimax. Peggy Marsh had no idea of what to do with success. She might have travelled around the world, but she

was the kind of person who preferred to stay at home.
Typically, she continued to worry about her financial
security, in spite of the fact that the film had given *Gone with
the Wind* a new lease of life. She even decided not to replace
a fur coat that had been stolen from her apartment during
one of her trips to the mountains.

The coming of the war gave her a new purpose in life.
Like so many celebrities, she flung herself into selling war
bonds.

Yet she still found herself haunted by vague forebodings
about the future. This seemed justified when she was asked
to launch a cruiser called the USS *Atlanta,* and the ship was
sunk off Guadalcanal a few months later with the loss of all
hands. But she worked hard on selling war bonds and, for
the first time since the publication of *Gone with the Wind,*
began to feel balanced and normal. Just as in the old days,
her home was filled with young soldiers. It became known
that she always replied to servicemen's letters, and she was
flooded with correspondence. She spent a great deal of time
at a nearby Red Cross canteen, mothering the soldiers and
sewing buttons on their uniforms. It would probably be fair
to say that Peggy Marsh enjoyed the war more than the
success of *Gone with the Wind.*

With the death of her father – after a long illness – in June
1944, and then the end of the war, she began to think about
the possibility of writing another book. Now she no longer
had to mother young servicemen, life seemed empty, and
she began to suffer from bouts of depression. But she had
used up all her subject matter. The only idea for a novel that
she noted down was about the impact of sudden fame on a
female novelist. She finally came to terms with the fact that
she would never return to her typewriter. Even the
unexpected reappearance of *Gone with the Wind* at the
bottom of the best-seller list did little to cheer her up.

John Marsh was beginning to show signs of a curious

illness that doctors had once diagnosed as psychosomatic. Now he had a fever that failed to respond to medicines. And during Christmas 1945 he had a heart attack in a remote hotel, and had to be rushed into hospital. From now on, he was a semi-invalid.

One of the problems that trailed in the wake of success was a lack of any major purpose to keep her occupied. This probably explains why she tended to become obsessive about small matters. She could suddenly explode angrily at old friends if she felt they wanted to exploit her. Her closest friend of Smith College days, Ginny Morris, had written to her asking if she could do a story about her for a magazine called *Photoplay*. Ginny needed the money to take her daughter, who suffered from breathing problems, to a milder climate. Peggy wrote her an irritable reply declaring that she hated publicity, and the idea of 'I-knew-her-when' articles. When she learned that autographed copies of *Gone with the Wind* were selling at a great deal more than the original $3 price, she was furious, and refused to allow Macmillan to publish an edition with her rubber-stamped autograph in it. 'I feel pretty violently about autographs and always have.' This was flatly untrue – she had autographed literally thousands of copies. She went on: 'When a stranger asks me for an autograph I feel just like he (or she) had asked me for a pair of my step-ins [knickers]. If I could bring back every autographed copy and destroy it, I would . . .' After the war, she obsessively pursued European publishers who had issued her book under Nazi occupation, although she was certainly in no need of the money.

By 1948, *Gone with the Wind* was still selling well, yet fan mail had virtually stopped. The reason seemed to be that most people assumed that the authoress was either very old or dead. One fortunate result was that she no longer had to protect her privacy with such paranoid obsessiveness.

Red Upshaw had not kept his promise to see her face to face

again. Occasionally, Peggy heard stories about how he had spent the war years in the Merchant Marine, and had become an incurable alcoholic. Then, in January 1949, she received a press cutting from Galveston, Texas, that stated that Berrien Kinnard Upshaw had been killed in a fall from the fifth-floor fire escape of a cheap hotel. The day before his death, he had suffered some kind of fit, and when he recovered, could no longer remember his name. At six in the morning, he walked out of the hotel room that he was sharing with three other men and onto the fire escape. Whether he jumped off the fire escape, or suffered another fit and fell, will never be known. Now, at last, Peggy Marsh could be certain that the secret of her marriage to the original Rhett Butler would never be revealed in her lifetime.

She occupied her days nursing her husband, who could only walk with difficulty. They hired a film projector, and spent a great deal of their time watching old movies – they watched virtually all the major Charlie Chaplins in the course of a few weeks.

On a stiflingly hot summer evening, 11 August 1949, Peggy and her husband set out to walk to the nearby Arts Theatre to see a film. Peggy had been depressed all day, and now went out without bothering to change out of the cotton house dress she was wearing. They parked opposite the theatre and then began crossing the road. It was a dangerous thing to do, because there was no level crossing and no traffic lights nearby. Moreover, a bend in the road prevented pedestrians from seeing approaching traffic. As they started slowly across, with her hand under John's elbow, a car came speeding down the street. Realizing that it was likely to hit them, she screamed, and ran back to the pavement, leaving her husband in the middle of the road. It was a bad decision. The driver of the car swerved to avoid John, hit Peggy Marsh, and dragged her along for seven feet before he stopped.

In the hospital, doctors discovered that she had a skull fracture that ran from her brain to the top of her spine. Five days later she died. She was forty-eight years old. The driver of the car, a taxi driver who had several convictions for reckless driving, was charged with driving while drunk, and released on bail of more than $5,000.

Strangely enough, Margaret Mitchell had always had a conviction that she would die in a car accident.

Chapter Eleven

Black Marries White: The Romance of Seretse Khama

The African version of the Duke of Windsor crisis began in London, in June 1947, when Seretse Khama, prince, descended from a life of noble chieftains stretching back to the seventeenth century, saw Ruth Williams: office clerk, daughter of a commercial traveller, across a dance floor.

Ever since birth, Seretse (meaning 'Red Earth') had been groomed for his future role as king. This was a time when African countries were moving towards independence from their colonial rulers, and it was essential that he should be well prepared to lead when the time came. He had been sent to the best schools and colleges in Africa, and then went on to Balliol College, Oxford, to study law. And it was when he was finishing his degree at the London bar that one evening, at a dance at his hall of residence, he met the pretty blonde from south London.

A year later, in October 1948, Prince Seretse horrified the British Foreign Office by announcing that he was marrying an English girl. Mixed marriages were still uncommon in Britain, but they were accepted. But in the southern part of Africa where Botswana (then Bechuanaland) lies, inter-racial marriage was political dynamite.

It was not that the people of Botswana minded having a white queen; after the initial shock they were perfectly happy about it. It was true that she was not of the same social class as their prince, but since he said he was in love and would not give her up, they accepted his decision. The problem lay with their neighbours, the white apartheid-minded governments in Rhodesia and the Republic of South Africa, who absolutely refused to tolerate the union. If the king of a neighbouring country set such an example, what sort of message would it send to the people of their own countries? The consequences were unthinkable.

The problem was more than a local affair because Botswana was a British protectorate, and the decision whether to allow Seretse to take up his throne with a white queen lay with the British government. Whilst not wishing to endorse racism, Britain was reluctant to offend important trading partners. Behind closed doors at the Foreign Office, it was also understood that the Republic of South Africa and Rhodesia might well take the opportunity to invade Botswana if Ruth became queen. Both countries had long sought to annex mineral-rich Botswana, and for decades Britain had firmly resisted their demands to hand the country over, since the people of Botswana objected strongly: 'Would the rabbit put his head into the mouth of the python?' they asked.

When he met Ruth, the twenty-six-year-old Seretse was a well-built, handsome young man, intelligent, courteous and modest, but also painfully shy with women. Unlike most of the other students, he had never had a girlfriend, and it was with considerable effort that he screwed up his courage to to cross the floor and ask Ruth to dance. Although the couple later dismissed reports that it was 'love at first sight', it was true that they quickly found that they shared many interests, including sport and jazz.

During the next few months they spent a great deal of time together. In Ruth, Seretse found the kind of companionship and understanding that had been lacking in his previous life. His parents had died when he was young, and he had been brought up by relatives in an atmosphere of inter-tribal rivalry. He was always aware that he had enormous responsibilities ahead of him. This is why he studied hard, although he greatly preferred football to Latin. Much of his youth had been spent in boarding school, returning during the holidays to sit at the tribal council beside his uncle Tshekedi, who was to rule until Seretse came of age.

Ruth was two years Seretse's junior. She had been born and brought up in the London suburb of Blackheath. The Second World War broke out when she was sixteen, and she was evacuated to the Surrey countryside to avoid the bombing. She became ill, and was sent back to her family in London, so that she witnessed the blitz. She decided to study domestic science, and enrolled at the London Polytechnic. But during food rationing, there was not enough food to continue the course; instead she joined the Women's Auxillary Air Force, driving supply trucks and ambulances. At the end of the war she had started work in an office for a Lloyds insurance company in the City. Two years later, she went with her sister to a dance organized by the London Missionary Society, where she met her future husband.

During the courtship they did the things most young couples do, going to the cinema and theatres, or on long country walks at weekends. Then, in June 1948, exactly a year after they had first met, Seretse asked her to marry him. She accepted, and they began to make arrangements at the beginning of September. By now Seretse had moved to a small flat in Camden Hill Gardens, south of Notting Hill Gate, the marriage was booked for 2 October at St George's, the church at the end of the road.

Ruth's father disapproved of his prospective son-in-law, and the plan to take Ruth back to Africa. It was also clear that Seretse's uncle would oppose the marriage: a prince

The Romance of Seretse Khama

Seretse Khama, Chief of the Bamangwato tribe,
with his English wife Ruth

was expected choose a wife – or wives – from the aristocratic tribal families. Seretse also anticipated difficulty from the tribal council, who could deprive him of the right to rule. In spite of all this, they determined to marry.

In mid-September 1948, Seretse summoned up courage and wrote to his uncle. He made it clear that giving up Ruth was not an option, but concluded: 'I shall return home whenever you say and will serve in any capacity.' When the old man received the sixpenny airmail letter ten days later, he was inspecting the site for a new college, with the British High Commissioner, who later said, 'he had a face like a fiddle when he showed me the letter.' They jumped into their vehicles and rushed to the post office, where Tshekedi cabled Seretse and the High Commissioner informed the Foreign Office of the 'problem'.

Tshekedi's telegram to Seretse said 'Get ready to leave at a moment's notice. I can only discuss your proposal personally after your arrival here.' Seretse knew if he returned home without marrying Ruth he might not be allowed to see her for a long time. So on 24 September, the couple explained the urgency of their position to their vicar and he agreed to marry them the next day. But in the meantime, the Foreign Office contacted the London Missionary Society, who in turn contacted the Bishop of London, who in turn persuaded the vicar to postpone the wedding.

So when the couple arrived at church with two witnesses, they were told that the wedding was cancelled. Ruth, who had given up her lodgings, demanded, 'Does the church want to force me to live in sin?' The answer, apparently, was yes. But the ceremony finally took place in secret a few days later at Kensington Register Office.

The story soon leaked, and next day newspapers carried the headlines: 'Ruler-to-be Weds Office Girl' (*Daily Mirror*); and 'Marriage That Rocks Africa' (*Daily Mail*). The *Mail* continued: 'Cecil Rhodes may have changed the whole history of Africa, but the London typist by marrying her African chief, has reversed the traditional black-white situation, and threatens to disrupt social and political relations in all Southern Africa.'

The British government found itself in an alarming position. Apart from wanting to avoid the possibility of an armed incursion into Botswana, it could not afford to offend South Africa. It relied upon South African gold being sold through the Bank of England (in dollars) to repay wartime loans to America; and South African uranium supplied Britain's developing atomic power industry. Acceptance of Seretse's chieftainship and marriage would challenge the whole philosophical basis of apartheid, (i.e. that not only was segregation natural but that it was desired by the masses themselves) which was the centrepiece of South Africa's newly elected National Party government's policy. Mixed marriages were strictly outlawed. If Seretse became king, National Party supporters threatened not only to break with the Commonwealth, but also to nationalize British holdings, such as gold mines, in South Africa.

Britain decided to play for time. Privately it was hoped that, with such wide cultural differences (and the possibility that Ruth was simply a 'gold digger') the marriage would soon collapse. The excuse the Foreign Office used was that Seretse's uncle and his followers were firmly opposed to the marriage, and that Britain was merely trying to prevent tribal unrest. But when Seretse returned home and appeared before the tribal council, he received overwhelming support for his enthronement with Ruth as queen. Four thousand elders voted for him, with only forty against. At this point Tshekedi left sadly, saying from now on he would be a private citizen.

So Botswana had no ruler. Seretse could not take up his hereditary position without approval from Britain, and this was withheld while a commission was appointed to look into the whole question. The country was put under direct colonial rule until the matter was resolved.

In the meantime, Seretse and his wife moved to Serowe, the capital of Botswana. In Whitehall it was still hoped that failure of the marriage would solve the problem. Surely, they reasoned, Ruth would never be able to adapt to the African way of life? The South African ambassador to London bet a substantial sum that she would not last six months, living among people whose principal symbol of wealth and prestige was cattle, and whose largest city was a collection of thatched huts.

But they were wrong. Ruth settled in surprisingly quickly. It was true she would not give up some of her western habits, such as going about in slacks, which raised eyebrows (being not at all acceptable for African women at that time), but she immediately set about learning the local language: giving tea to the numerous visitors who called at their bungalow and making friends with her royal relatives. A British civil servant who met her reported back to London: 'Ruth Khama is a nice looking girl, much nicer looking than her photographs – pretty golden hair . . . She was simply dressed, and conversed freely and intelligently. In fact, she is a tougher proposition than we hoped she might be – she will never be bought off.'

In December 1949 the official inquiry concluded that although the tribal election had been properly convened and conducted, Seretse Khama was 'not a fit and proper person to discharge the function of chief'. It went on to recommend recognition of Seretse only 'if conditions changed', which meant if Ruth and Seretse got divorced.

Next, it was decided to invite Seretse to London and to offer him an annual allowance in return for abdication. He was told (untruthfully) that no decision had been made about his future, and that he was being invited to take part

The Romance of Seretse Khama

In May 1979, years after his return from exile, Seretse again managed to outrage the South African government. At a meeting of African heads of state, the question of Namibia's independance from South Africa was being dicussed. The Namibian pro-independence movement SWAPCO was arguing for a South African surrender of power without an election. Seretse argued that this was not democratic and would lead to South Africa refusing to co-operate . . .

'I don't want SWAPCO to be blamed for the collapse of negotiations. I want South Africa to be regarded as the nigger in the woodpile.'

This choice of phrase amused the African leaders, but infuriated Pik Botha, the South African foreign minister, who called it 'an insult' and attempted (unsuccessfully) to create a diplomatic incident out of the matter.

in discussions. In a personal dispatch to Whitehall, the British High Commissioner noted that Seretse would be more likely to agree to abdication in the 'calm atmosphere' of London, and that if he refused, it would be better that he should not be in Botswana when the decision not to allow him to rule was announced.

Ruth was invited to accompany her husband, but she refused to go, suspecting that she would not be allowed to return; she was by now expecting a child and the couple wanted the heir to the Khama line to be born in Botswana. Seretse left cheerfully, dismissing her doubts.

At the Colonial Office in Whitehall, Seretse was offered

Seretse and Ruth Khama with their children, 1956

£800 per annum to give up the throne and live abroad. He later recalled: 'I was speechless. His calm unemotional manner was as unfeeling as if he were asking me to give up smoking.' Seretse declined unless his people were consulted; but this was refused. Soon afterwards the Cabinet met and decided to withhold recognition of Seretse and to exile him for five years. The telegram Seretse sent to Ruth summed up the situation: 'Tribe and myself tricked by British government. I am banned from whole protectorate. Love Seretse.'

Then, for the first time, he decided to speak to the press, and called a conference. In no time the story was international headline news. Only the South African press welcomed the British government's decision. The British public, predictably, showed itself firmly in favour of romance, and fully supported the couple and the people of Botswana, who wanted Seretse to return as their king.

It would probably have been better for the British government to admit the reasons for their action; instead, they categorically denied that there had been any communication with South Africa over the issue – which was obviously untrue. Although there were protests in the House of Commons debate which followed – particularly over the dishonourable way Seretse had been tricked into exile – the policy now stood.

In Botswana the people were outraged and their reaction was to boycott the assembly called by the colonial administration to make the announcement. The world's press gathered in force at the tiny capital of Serowe, to see the High Commissioner dressed in full regalia with white feathers on top of his solar topee, addressing an almost empty meeting ground.

While Seretse had become the centre of press attention in London, Ruth was the centre of press attention in Scrowe. Both reacted with great restraint. A South African journalist who had interviewed Seretse before his unexpected notoriety, now reported, 'I more than half expected that all this ballyhoo would have gone to his head . . . but I found him the same quiet, modest chap.'

In Serowe reporters were equally impressed by a calm and collected Ruth, now one of the most publicized women in the world, who offered them a choice of teas.

Eventually, when the fuss had died down, Seretse was allowed to return to Botswana for a brief visit, to sort out his financial affairs and witness the birth of his child. The condition was that he should remain out of the public eye, and make no speeches. But when he arrived, he found that such a large crowd had gathered that he was obliged out of politeness to greet them, before asking them to disperse quietly. The District Commisioner was furious. But there was celebration in the Commonwealth Office when the Khamas' baby was born. Young officials ran up and down the corridors shouting, 'It's a girl! It's a GIRL!' A male heir might have caused a lot more trouble.

The Khamas left Botswana with their new baby, and for the next five years lived in London. Seretse resumed his law studies, and in due course another child was born. During this time the situation gradually changed in favour of Seretse's return home. He was not forgotten: there were many protests from groups in Britain and abroad and the people of Botswana never gave up hope, continuing to send letters of support, and petitions to the Queen. Seretse and Tshekedi were reconciled, and agreed that the best future for Botswana would be as a democratic nation with an elected government. And Ruth and her husband remained a human interest story that continued to prick the conscience of the West; in the 1950s they came to symbolize issues of racial discrimination, and were used as a stick to beat South Africa by opponents of apartheid.

As the end of Seretse's five-year exile approached, British officials admitted privately that they 'had a very bad conscience about Seretse'. The Prime Minister Clement Atlee remarked: 'It is as if we had been obliged to agree to Edward VII's abdication so as not to annoy the Irish Free State and the USA.'

The conditions which allowed for Seretse's return were beginning to emerge. South Africa's apartheid now aroused opposition around the world, and Britain was no longer so ready for appeasement. Britain was also gradually withdrawing from its role as a colonial power. Self-rule and financial independence of the colonies was the objective. Now, surveys showed that Botswana was rich in copper, coal and diamonds, and a system of elected government

On his return to Botswana Seretse found it galling to have his every move watched by Special Branch agents. The existence of a prominent 'mixed' couple in an otherwise segregated society was seen as the thin end of a dangerous wedge prising apart the basic racial assumptions of colonial rule. A ludicrous note was introduced into police surveillance by fears of a wave of black men marrying white women. Spies relayed in all seriousness the remark of a white woman in Francistown who leaned across the tea table in the Tati Hotel to ask Ruth if she 'could find a decent African husband for her'.

was in place. When, in October 1955, the tribal council refused to allow in an international prospecting company unless Seretse was returned, it was finally agreed that he would return as a private citizen, with the right to take part in politics.

So in 1956, eight years after their secret wedding, the Khamas were able to celebrate their anniversary in the house they had built overlooking Serowe. When they first moved in they had to suffer the attentions of Afrikaans-speaking sightseers who arrived in cars, some of whom even asked to see their double bed. But slowly things returned to normal, and Ruth, clad in a floral print dress, could be seen going shopping like any suburban housewife.

On his return as a private citizen, freed from the constraints of hereditary status, Seretse was able to realize greater individual potential. He could easily have become titular non-executive head of state after the death of his uncle in 1959, but instead he chose to lead a national political party and run for election. His overwhelming popularity guaranteed success, and in 1965 he became Prime Minister, and Executive President of the Republic of Botswana in the following year.

In July 1979, the Queen visited Botswana, and former London typist Ruth, as wife of the head of state, now found herself in the curious position of having precedence over the Queen at all formal events. Shortly after her arrival, Queen Elizabeth invested Seretse with his second knighthood. By the end of the 1960s Botswana became known as a model of non-racial democracy in an area of Africa noted for racial hatred and tension.

For the opponents of apartheid and racial discrimination, the model marriage of Seretse and Ruth Khama symbolized hope for the future.